BALAJI — VENKATESHWARA

Lord of Tirumala – Tirupati

An Introduction

To

Venkateshwara,
who has given me every happiness
and helped me through times of stress and sorrow,

and to

Chinny, Prashanth and Rudra,
my most accommodating and encouraging family,
whose pilgrimages on foot from Madras to Tirumala
have reaffirmed my faith.

BALAJI – VENKATESHWARA

Lord of Tirumala – Tirupati
An Introduction

Nanditha Krishna

Vakils, Feffer and Simons Ltd.
Hague Building, 9, Sprott Road, Ballard Estate,
Mumbai 400 001

First printing 2000

Price in India Rs. 295/-

Published by Mrs. Jean Trindade
for Vakils, Feffer and Simons Ltd.
Hague Building, 9, Sprott Road, Ballard Estate
Mumbai 400 001, India

Printed by Arun K. Mehta at Vakil & Sons Ltd.
Industry Manor, Appasaheb Marathe Marg,
Worli, Mumbai 400 025, India

ISBN   81-87111-46-1

Contents

Acknowledgements

To Dr. I. V. Subba Rao, I.A.S., Executive Officer, Mr. A. Subhas Goud P.R.O., Mr. V. Chandrasekhara Naidu, Superintendent, P.R.O. Office, Mr. P. N. Jayasekhar, Assistant Photographer, and Mr. V. Ramachandra, Assistant in the P.R.O.'s Office, of the Tirumala Tirupati Devasthanam, who gave me access, information, photographs and whatever help I asked for, and to Mr. Surendra Babu of the Indian Express, Tirupati, for introducing me to these wonderful people,

To the artist Y. Venkatesh, who learned to draw in the traditional style of Tirupati art to produce the beautiful drawings in this book, and to the staff of the C.P. Ramaswami Aiyar Foundation and its constituents — Y. Rushendra Kumar, H. Manikandan, M. Amirthalingam, Christina Isaac, K. Shantha, S. Sumathra, S. Gowri, Malathi Narasimhan, S.P. Vijayakumari, R. Shiva, S. Ravi and V. Shanmugam— who helped me in so many ways,

To Mr. V.K. Rajamani, for the cover and other colour photos, Mrs. Sharada Rajamani who shared her knowledge of the God of Tirumala, to Mr. M. Parthasarathi who gave me the photograph of the original image and to Mr. P. Sudhakar who provided some of the other photos,

To Mr. Arun Mehta, who suggested the book, and Mrs. Sudha Mehta, of Vakil & Sons Ltd., both wonderful friends and people, who were so helpful and co-operative,

To Mrs. Rajeshree Sabnis, Mr. S. Sivagurunathan, Mr. Satish Nagwekar, Mr. M. Annamalai and Mr. Parag Chemburkar for their competence and enthusiasm in scanning and correcting the photographs and laying out the text,

To my mother Shakunthala Jagannathan, an eminent writer herself, for proof reading the book, and, to my father A.R. Jagannathan, who taught me to have faith and belief in Venkateshwara,

To Chinny, Prashanth and Rudra, who encouraged me through times of creativity and frustration,

Thank you very much.

Preface

Balaji — Venkateshwara has been by my side from the moment I entered this world. As our family deity, he received the hair from my first tonsure, my two sons' several tonsures, and every vow and pilgrimage was made in his name. My husband and sons have frequently walked to Tirumala from Madras and I, myself, have walked up the hill and visited Tirumala several times. After every wedding in the family, including my own, we would perform a kalyana utsavam at Tirumala. Venkatesha has been so intricately woven into my life that his picture adorns every room in my house.

Thus when Mr. Arun Mehta of Vakil and Sons Ltd. called and asked me to write a book on the Lord of Tirumala-Tirupati, I was ecstatic, for I believe that it could only have been Venkatesha himself who wanted me to write it. Thereafter, things began to happen. I had no material to start with, except my grandmother's tales and a few children's comics on the subject. Suddenly, I started receiving gifts of old and new books on Venkateshwara and Tirumala-Tirupati from unexpected sources, from people I hardly knew and had not met for years, and who did not know I was writing a book on the subject. Today I have one of the best libraries on Balaji, a veritable cornucopia of material which has made it possible for me to write this book. This is one of the many miracles of Balaji. For the rest I went to Tirupati, where the Executive Officer and staff were most helpful.

Although this is the story of one God and his temple, his mysterious origins, the miracles and legends associated with him, the sanctity of the hill, peaks and lakes, the elaborate rituals and festivals, his beautiful jewellery, his renowned powers to do the impossible, all provide a wealth of material about the God and attract millions of pilgrims to the temple. The various images in the temple, the temple itself and the sculptures which adorn it pale, in contrast, into insignificance. In spite of the inaccessibility of the temple, pilgrims flock in large numbers to have darshan and to participate in the daily, weekly and seasonal festivals. His popularity knows no bounds. All these have made Venkateshwara into one of the most popular Gods of 20th century Hinduism, definitely the wealthiest. What makes the temple so popular, and what are the beliefs of the people, are questions that I have tried to answer.

I have tried to present to the reader the flavour of Tirumala, a curious combination of myth and reality, a remnant of geological, historical and legendary events of the past preserved in a remote sanctuary atop a hill, and how it finds relevance in the present day. The story of creation, the appearance of the hill and the clearing of the forests, as narrated in this book, are legendary accounts of geographic and historic events, known to our people several millennia ago.

To re-create the atmosphere of Tirumala–Tirupati, the legends associated with the God and the temple have been illustrated in the Tirupati style of drawing, a school of art synonymous with Kalamkari painting and executed with vegetable colours. It is still extremely popular in the region of Tirupati–Kalahasti in Chitoor district of Andhra Pradesh.

A little-known fact is that the temple is a source of so much charity and education, keeping contemporary requirements to the forefront. Every coin dropped in the hundi goes to help a worthy cause.

Tirumala also represents the cultural unity of India : It is a Tamil deity and tradition situated in Andhra Pradesh, a God with a name (Balaji) of North Indian origin, a manifestation of a pan-Indian deity (Vishnu) and his incarnation, whose feminine aspect resides in Maharashtra.

While the material in this book has been well researched, I have presented it in, I hope, a reader-friendly way for the layman, the devotee and the curious who wish to know more about this phenomenon. Folk stories and oral traditions have been woven into Sanskrit traditions to present popular perceptions. Diacritical marks over Sanskrit and Tamil words have been omitted as they are unknown to the lay reader.

As we move towards the new millennium, one's thoughts turn to the future — what does it have in store for us, how will it be different? The answers lie in the past, in the antiquity and continuity of Indian culture, and in the strength and resilience of the Hindu religion which provides eternal values and belief systems which have stood the test of time.

January 2000
Chennai 600 018   Nanditha Krishna

viii

Vinaa Venkatesham na naatho na naathah
Sadaa Venkatesham smaraami smaraami
Hare Venkatesha prasiddha prasiddha
Priyam Venkatesha prayachchha prayachchha

There is no Lord for me other than Venkatesha
I think of Venkatesha all the time
May Venkatesha be happy with my prayers
May Venkatesha be pleased to bless me forever

The Lord of Tirumala   Chapter 1

The Lord of Tirumala is like a magnet, drawing people
to his temple on the hill. Every day, thousands of
devotees flock to his shrine in reverence and love. The
stories of his miracles and compassion are legion. Who is
this God? Why is he so beloved of all? To know and
understand this phenomenon, we have to go back in time
to the ancient Varaha Purana, a book which contains the
story of the manifestation of Lord Vishnu as Balaji or
Venkatesha, Lord of the Tirumala hill.

Brahma, Vishnu and Shiva — the Trinity of Creator,
Preserver and Destroyer — are, themselves,
manifestations of the formless, all-powerful and
omnipresent Supreme Being. Vishnu, as the protector
of the cosmos, preserves life, making sure that all
creatures enjoy a meaningful existence. Whenever Dharma
or the Righteous Law is threatened, he appears on
earth as an incarnation or a manifestation, to protect the
good and his devotees.

Venkateshwara or Balaji is one such manifestation, and
the *sanctum sanctorum* which houses the Lord on the
Tirumala hills is known as Shri Vaikuntham, the heavenly
abode of Vishnu.

This, then, is the story of Balaji Venkateshwara, Lord of
Tirumala-Tirupati.

Brahma, Shiva and Vishnu, the
Hindu Trinity of Creator, Destroyer
and Preserver.

Varaha rescues the earth

For eight thousand yugas — a day and night of the Creator Brahma — Surya the sun belched fire, burning the hills and forests to ashes. There was no rain, so the holy sages left the earth and sought refuge in the heavens. Then Vayu the wind blew with all his might for many years till huge clouds were formed, which rained incessantly and caused a great flood. The Earth sank into Patalaloka, the nether world, where she remained for a thousand yugas, a part of the night of Brahma. It was the pralaya, the primeval flood, which submerged the entire earth under water.

On that huge sheet of water, Vishnu lay on a ficus leaf as the eternal child, Vatapatrashayi. Seeing the plight of Mother Earth at the bottom of the waters, he assumed the frightening form of Shweta Varaha, the White Boar, and descended into the nether world to search for her. The evil demon Hiranyaksha attacked him, and they fought a long and violent battle, at the end of which Varaha destroyed the demon with his mighty tusks. He then lifted up Mother Earth on his tusks and emerged from the waters. Placing a foot on the divine snake Adishesha, with Mother Earth on his tusks, he dazzled the whole world with his majestic appearance. The holy sages recited the hymns from the ancient books of wisdom and knowledge, the Vedas, and requested Varaha to bring Mother Earth back to her original glory.

Varaha then re-established Mother Earth, delineated the limits of the seven seas (sapta sagaras) and the seven continents (sapta lokas), and requested Brahma to re-create life on earth. To protect his devotees, he decided to live on earth and asked Garuda, his vehicle, the man-eagle, to bring the divine hill Kridachala from Vaikuntha, his heavenly abode, to establish his new home on earth.

Varaha selected a location which was sixty yojanas (960 kilometres) south of the river Gomati, five yojanas (80 kilometres) west of the eastern sea (Bay of Bengal) and adjoining the Swarnamukhi river. Here Garuda brought Kridachala, a sacred hill three yojanas (48 kilometres) wide and thirty yojanas (480 kilometres) long. As its shape resembled Sesha, Lord Narayana's thousand-hooded snake, it was called Seshadri. It was heaven on earth, with flowering plants and fruit-bearing trees, with peaks of gold and precious stones, where birds sang and kinnaras (celestial musicians) sang and danced, a veritable paradise.

Varaha occupied a temple on the western side of the sacred pool, the Swami Pushkarni. But his appearance with the tusks and weapons was so frightening, that Brahma, the Gods, the Saptarishis (seven sages) and other celestials prayed to Vishnu, requesting him to assume a more peaceful form and live on the hill to protect his people.

Thereafter, the supreme, lotus-eyed Vishnu, holding the shankha (conch), chakra (discus) and gada (mace), descended to the Seshadri hill. With Bhudevi (Mother Earth) and Lakshmi (the Goddess of Prosperity), two aspects of the Supreme Mother Goddess, by his side, he settled under the divya vimana (dome) to grant the prayers of the people.

Brahma promised the gods and the sages that Varaha would stay on Seshadri hill till the end of the Shweta Varaha kalpa (the present age), as it was as wonderful as heaven or Vaikuntha.

Thus goes the narration in the Venkatachala Mahatmyam of the Varaha Purana by sage Suta, when requested by Saunaka and others to enlighten them on the places sacred to Lord Vishnu.

Vishnu of the Tirumala or Venkatadri hills is known as Venkatesha or Venkateshwara (Lord of Venkata), the destroyer of sins and the giver of prosperity.

Another name by which he is revered is Srinivasa, in whom the Goddess of Prosperity, Sri or Lakshmi, dwells.

In the north of India he is known as Balaji because when the world was immersed under the waters, Vishnu, as a newborn child, floated on a leaf on the waters. He is Narayana, the Creator, Destroyer and the Refuge. Another meaning for Balaji is Universal Mother.

He is addressed as Perumal (the Great Lord), Malaiyappa (Lord of the hill) and Govinda (a name of Lord Krishna) by his devotees as they inch forward through the temple, calling out to the holy image of their Lord.

Vishnu as Balaji, the child floating on the waters of the great flood; calendar painting

Venkateshwara with Sridevi and Bhudevi — bronze utsava murtis.

The Pilgrimage

The Tirumala hill forms the southern end of the Eastern Ghats. It rises to a maximum height of 1104 metres above sea level and consists of seven peaks or ridges, whence the name Saptagiri or seven hills. It covers an area of about 250 square kilometres and resembles a massive serpent or dragon, giving it the name Seshadri or the hill of the snake. The head of the serpent is Tirumala, the body is Ahobilam to the north and the tail is Srisailam, even further north.

The Tirumala hill

The temple is approached from the town of Tirupati by a ghat road. Once upon a time, the only way to reach the temple was by a footpath eleven kilometers long, crossing thick jungles and the seven peaks. It is a charming and breath-taking walk through a thickly forested hill, commencing at the entrance tower or Alipiri (Adipadi or steps). The difficult sections are at the beginning, from Alipiri to the Gali Gopuram, and at the end, near the top, known as the "knee breaker".

The nearest railhead, bus terminus or airport, to reach the temple, are at Tirupati, the town at the foot of the hills, in the southern Indian state of Andhra Pradesh. From Tirupati there are regular bus and taxi services, managed by the Tirumala Tirupati Devasthanam, to go up the hill. The temple can either be approached by road — there are two separate roads for uphill and downhill traffic — or by foot along the lovely eleven kilometer-long footpath with canopied steps traversing the hills. Walking up the hills is more difficult but confers great merit, for the hill is nearly as sacred as the temple.

Accommodation of all varieties is provided by the Tirumala Tirupati Devasthanam, from free to low-cost to air-conditioned and expensive rooms and cottages. Free meals are also provided to all who desire it. It is a miracle how well organized the arrangements are, considering

A view of the hill from the beginning of the footpath at the Alipiri tower

the millions of pilgrims who visit Tirumala every day. In spite of the crowds, the hilltop is kept scrupulously clean.

No visit to Tirumala is complete without a visit to the temple of Padmavati, the consort of Venkateshwara, at Tiruchanur, formerly known as Tiruchokinur or Tiruchukanur. The story of their divine union is deeply entwined with the story of the hills.

Pilgrims flock in millions to the temple of Venkateshwara in the Tirumala or Venkatadri hills, above the town of Tirupati, to be rid of their sins and to be blessed with prosperity. He is probably the most popular God of contemporary Hinduism and is credited with innumerable miracles and immense spiritual power.

A sizeable number of his devotees are Muslims, for a former Nawab of Gandikota in Cuddapah district, Andhra Pradesh, was an ardent devotee of Lord Venkateshwara. His daughter refused to marry, and died dreaming of her beloved Lord Balaji who, she believed, would marry her after her death. Between 5 and 10 percent of the devotees are Muslims.

This is the story of how Vishnu came to reside on Venkatadri hill, to look after his devotees and to save good from evil during Kali yuga, the age we live in.

There are many stories associating Vishnu with the Tirumala or Venkatadri hills.

Vishnu comes to Venkatadri hill

According to the Bhavishyottara Purana, Vishnu remained on Venkatadri for the first three yugas — Krita, Treta and Dvapara. At the beginning of the present yuga — the Kali yuga — he decided to leave for Vaikuntha, his heaven, with his spouse Sri or Lakshmi, the Goddess of Prosperity.

Learning of this, sage Narada went to Brahma who, also, felt that while Vishnu remained on earth people were pious and meritorious. Accordingly, he raised a tamarind tree on Venkatadri hill, beneath which he formed an anthill. Narada was instructed to bring Vishnu back to Venkatadri, to reside in the anthill.

Narada went to the banks of the river Ganga where the rishis or sacred sages were performing rituals. He asked them to whom they would dedicate the fruits of their prayers. The rishis discussed the matter, but could not arrive at any decision.

Lakshmi, Kolhapur temple, Maharashtra.

Bhrigu rishi first went to Satyaloka. Here he met Brahma. Bhrigu behaved rudely and was ignored. Angered, he went to Kailasa, where Shiva was in the company of his consort Parvati. Disapproving, Bhrigu left for Vaikuntha where he saw Vishnu reclining on the serpent Adishesha, with Lakshmi by his side. Bhrigu went up to Vishnu and kicked him on the right chest, the abode of Lakshmi. Vishnu got up, bowed to the rishi, washed the latter's hands and feet and pressed them. He apologized for his inactivity and gratified Bhrigu so much that Bhrigu returned to the banks of the river Ganga and informed the other rishis that they should pray to Vishnu for salvation.

Meanwhile Lakshmi was very angry that Vishnu had pacified and apologized to the rishi who had kicked her abode on his chest. She would no longer live on his chest but go to Karaveera Kshetram (Kolhapur in Maharashtra) where she would henceforth reside.

The unhappy Vishnu then left Vaikuntha to return to Venkatadri, where he lived incognito in the anthill. During this period, Dvapara yuga came to an end and Kali yuga began.

Lakshmi knew that Vishnu was living in an anthill on Venkatachala. She took the appearance of a milkmaid and Brahma and Shiva that of a cow and calf respectively. She sold them to the Chola queen who ruled over the Venkatachala region, knowing that the cow would take care of her Lord.

Every day, the cow and calf accompanied the Chola king's head of two thousand cattle to graze on the hillside. But unknown and unnoticed by the others, she would go up the hill and empty her milk on the anthill, over Vishnu. Noticing the lack of milk, the cowherd followed the cow up the hill and observed it emptying its milk over the anthill. Furious, he threw his stick at the cow, but Vishnu took the blow and saved the cow. Amazed at the phenomenon, the cowherd fell dead.

The Chola king went to Venkatachala to investigate, and was cursed by Vishnu to become a demon to expiate his servant's sin. The king prayed for mercy, so Vishnu relented and informed him that he would have to suffer the curse till he was reborn as Akasha Raja, and would gain merit when his daughter Padmavati married Venkatesha.

As Vishnu searched the hill for the herbs recommended by Brihaspati to cure his head-wound, he came across Varaha, his own incarnation. As he narrated the story of his return to Venkatadri, Varaha told him that he had hunted out and defeated the demon Vrishabhasura. He was very happy to see Vishnu back at Venkatadri.

Thereafter, Vishnu requested him for some place to live in till the end of Kali yuga. Varaha said that if Vishnu paid the price, he would measure out some land.

Vishnu replied that if Lakshmi, the Goddess of Wealth, was still living with him, he would have been affluent enough to pay the price, but since she had left and gone to Kolhapur, how could he earn the money? Since Varaha had rescued the earth from Patalaloka, he could mark out a space where the Lord would live. In return, Varaha would receive the first prayer and offering of food from Vishnu's devotees.

Varaha agreed and assigned a plot for Vishnu, as well as Vakulamalika to serve him food mixed with honey and to apply medicine on his wound, which healed in response to her devotion. Vakulamalika was actually Yashoda, the mother of Krishna in a previous life, now reborn to take care of Vishnu as Venkateshwara on Venkatachala and to see him as a Kalyana murti (divine bridegroom) in the Kali yuga.

Vakulamalika

9

Marriage of Venkatesha and Padmavati

After the Mahabharata war, the land of Thondaimandalam was ruled by Akasha Raja, whose capital was situated at Narayanapuram, near the Venkatachala hill range. As he was childless, he decided to perform a great sacrifice and, when the land was ploughed for the sacrifice, a thousand-petalled lotus containing a baby was discovered. She was an incarnation of Goddess Lakshmi and was named Padmavati, as she was born in a lotus.

The baby grew up into a beautiful young girl. One day, sage Narada appeared in court, read her palm and predicted that she would be the bride of Vishnu. The same day, Venkateshwara was chasing a wild elephant in the Venkatachala forest, and followed it into the royal garden where he met Padmavati, who fell in love with him. He returned home and enlightened Vakulamalika about his past birth as Rama and Lakshmi's as Sita, and how they would both be united in Kali yuga as Srinivasa and Padmavati.

Vakulamalika was keen on seeing Vishnu as a Kalyanamurti, and immediately offered to leave for Akasha Raja's city, and arrange the sacred marriage alliance.

Crossing the river Swarnamukhi, she reached the Shiva temple where she learned of Padmavati's encounter with a handsome young man. Vakulamalika requested for an audience with Padmavati's mother, Dharunidevi. Meanwhile, Venkateshwara disguised himself as a female Pulinda astrologer and entered the city, announcing her sooth-saying abilities. The astrologer then informed queen Dharunidevi that Padmavati, her daughter, had fallen in love with a handsome young man who was Srinivasa, the Lord of Venkatachala. She should be married to him immediately, or would collapse in three days. Also, as

proof, an old woman would soon arrive to discuss the marriage, he told the queen, and left.

As predicted, Vakulamalika soon approached the queen for the hand of Padmavati for Srinivasa. Dharunidevi discussed the subject with the king and the royal couple announced their approval. Sages Brihaspati and Shuka fixed up the auspicious time for the wedding and predicted auspiciousness and happiness for the young couple and the world through this marriage.

All the gods and the sages arrived at Venkatachala to witness the marriage. Vishwakarma, the divine architect, constructed a beautiful city on the hill and Lord Indra a beautiful mandapa (pavilion) for the wedding ceremony.

As the Goddess Lakshmi had left him, Venkatesha had no money to perform his wedding. So Venkatesha took a loan from Kubera, the God of Wealth, promising to repay him within a thousand years. To help him repay his dues, pilgrims still shower him with money. By helping their Lord, the devotees believe that their Lord will help them in return.

Invitations to the wedding were sent to all the inhabitants of the fourteen worlds, the Gods, Goddesses and the celestial beings. It was to be a grand affair, and all the celestials, accompanied by the apsaras, gandharvas and kinnaras descended on earth to perform the wedding of Venkatesha and Padmavati.

11

Then, riding his eagle-vehicle Garuda, Venkatesha set out in a glorious procession to Narayanapuram, accompanied by Lord Shiva on his bull and the other deities on their vehicles, preceded by the divine dancers and musicians, the Gandharvas and Apsaras, and followed by musical bands, while sages and seers recited the Vedas. As they passed the hermitage of Sukha Maharishi, the sage sang in wonder at the fantastic procession. He invited Venkatesha to come in and accept his offering of food. In return, the sage was asked how he expected to feed the vast procession. The sage replied that if he could satisfy the Lord, everyone else would automatically be satisfied. Pleased by the sage's devotion, Venkatesha entered the hermitage and accepted his offering of fruits. And all the processionists had a strange feeling of having had a good feast, without having eaten a single morsel of food.

They soon arrived at Narayanapuram where they were received by King Akasha Raja with music, flowers and sandalwood paste. Riding an elephant, Venkatesha entered the marriage hall where the wedding was performed according to Vedic rites by the sages Vashishtha and Brihaspati. Then, to the chanting of Vedic hymns by the sages and the singing of auspicious songs by the women, Srinivasa tied the mangala sutra around the neck of Padmavati, and the celestials rained flowers on the holy couple.

Later, Lakshmi, the consort of Vishnu, also joined Venkatesha on the hill. The Lord told her of his debt, to be paid with interest, to Kubera. To help him, she should enrich his devotees who would give him contributions of money and wealth. This would help him redeem his debt. Lakshmi agreed, and returned to live in his heart, whence his name Srinivasa, or the dwelling place of Sri or Lakshmi.

Venkatesha with Sridevi and
Bhudevi — bronze kalyana murtis.

That is why pilgrims offer money and precious jewels to
Srinivasa, to help him pay off his debt to Kubera and,
in return, earn great merit.

The Temple for Venkateshwara

After the death of Akasha Raja, his brother Thondaimaan
and son Vasudasa battled each other for the succession.
On the request of Padmavati, Srinivasa intervened and
divided the kingdom into two regions, leaving thirty two
villages for Padmavati, who was Akasha Raja's daughter.
But Srinivasa and Padmavati continued to live in sage
Agastya's hermitage.

One day, Thondaimaan came to Srinivasa and told him of
his desire to see the Lord frequently. Srinivasa then
suggested the construction of a shrine on the hill, on the
place allotted to him by Varaha on the banks of a
beautiful lake. Being an ardent devotee, Thondaimaan
built a temple with a tower, prakaras, cattle sheds, storage
space and more, added a foot path through the seven
peaks and renovated the flower well (Pushkarini).
The entire hill became a reconstruction of Vaikuntha,
Vishnu's heaven. Consecrated with Vedic hymns by the
Gods and the sages, the temple tower was named
Ananda Nilayam, the abode of happiness.

13

The Annual Festival of Tirumala

During the celebrations, Brahma took a promise from Srinivasa, that he would redeem the sins of all the pilgrims who came to the temple. Srinivasa agreed, and the Seshadri hills were renamed as Venkata (Vem = dire sins, kata = power of immunity). Srinivasa came to be known as Venkateshwara or Venkatesha, Lord of the Venkata hills.

Brahma lit two lamps with the instructions that they should burn continuously and that Srinivasa should live on the Venkata hills, granting boons to his devotees who came there. And to this, too, did Srinivasa agree.

Brahma then decided to arrange a grand celebration. He called Vishwakarma and ordered the preparation of chariots, vehicles, temple umbrellas and diamond ornaments, and gave Thondaimaan the work of making all other arrangements. All the kings of India were invited to this grand celebration.

The celebration began on the first day of the New Moon, in the month of Bhadrapada (Tamil Purattaasi) and went on for ten days. People came from every part of the country to witness it. They desired that it should be repeated every year. Thus it became an annual festival — the Brahmotsavam, the festival of Brahma.

After the celebration, Brahma returned to heaven, having fulfilled his mission of leaving Vishnu on the Venkata hills for the duration of Kali yuga.

Srinivasa turns into stone

With the progress of Kali yuga, the world was plunged into chaos and evil. Lord Srinivasa announced that with the chaotic rule of the human race in Kali yuga, he no longer wished to talk directly to the unworthy. He would become a stone statue and communicate only with his dear devotees.

Saying this, he transferred himself into a statue, now the stone icon of Venkateshwara, on Tirumala hill.

Once Srinivasa was no longer available to him, Thondaimaan lost interest in ruling. He handed over his kingdom to his son and left for Venkatadri. There he chanted the thousand names (sahasranaama) of the Lord with offerings of tulasi (sacred basil) leaves till he attained moksha or final liberation.

Miracles of Venkateshwara

Venkateshwara is credited with countless miracles performed to save and redeem his devotees.

Vasu, a great devotee of the Lord, was a tribal hunter. One day he went to the forest to collect honey to mix with the food he wanted to offer the Lord. Meanwhile, his only child, a twelve year old boy named Suveera, offered the food to Venkatesha and then ate it. When Vasu heard of this on his return, he was furious and wanted to kill his child. But Venkatesha appeared and stayed his hand, saying that Suveera too was his devotee, and he had happily accepted the offering without the honey.

A pious lady prayed to Venkatesha to save her sick husband's life, in return for which she would gift her mangal sutra (thaali), her wedding symbol which she wore around her neck, into the hundi (collection box). When the husband became well, she decided, instead, to buy another mangal sutra as her offering, and dropped it in the Lord's hundi. But when she came out of the temple, the thaali around her neck was missing. Venkateshwara, who had saved her husband's life, had redeemed her pledge.

Hathiram Bhava was a Bengali devotee who came to the hill to worship Venkatesha. He built an ashram where he lived alone, and was known as Sevadasji. As his mode of worship was mystical and different, he was avoided by the others. So the Lord visited him every night and they would play a game of chess together. One night the Lord left his pearl necklace in the house of Sevadas. When Sevadas took it to the temple in the morning, his story was not believed, and he was imprisoned for theft. Sevadas prayed to the Lord to prove his innocence. At midnight, a white elephant entered the prison cell. The terrified jailers ran and brought the temple authorities. When they opened the prison doors, the elephant vanished before their eyes, leaving them dumbfounded. Sevadas ran to the temple shouting "Hathiram" (hathi=elephant). His innocence was established and he came to be known as Hathiram Mahant.

A poor man had nothing to offer the Lord except the two rupees left in his pocket. He put that in the hundi, and came home to find that he had won a gold ring in a chit fund.

The stories of Venkatesha's miracles are endless and a few appear in some of the following chapters. Venkateshwara is the fountainhead of compassion, and the true devotee is never denied his Lord's grace.

The Sacred Hill   Chapter 3

The Tirumala hill is believed to be Kridadri or Kridachala, as sacred as Vaikuntha, Vishnu's heaven, having once been situated in heaven. Known by different names in the different yugas, it was called Vrishabhadri or Vrishabhachala in Krita yuga, Anjanadri or Anjanachala in Treta yuga, Seshadri or Seshachala in Dvapara yuga and Venkatadri or Venkatachala in Kali yuga. The stories of the hill establish its sanctity in every age. The word Tirumala itself means sacred hill : Tiru (pronounced thiru) = Shri, meaning sacred, and mala (Telugu, pronounced malaa), or malai (Tamil) means hill. Achala and adri are suffixes meaning hill.

Vrishabhadri : During the Krita yuga, a wicked asura named Vrishabhasura captured the Kridadri hill where he performed a terrible penance for five thousand years, frightening the holy men living there. Every day he would cut off his head and offer it along with a flower to Lord Narasimha, while his head would grow back again.

Finally, Narayana appeared before him and asked him what he wanted. Vrishabhasura replied that he wanted no boon but wished to fight with the God. Thus began a terrible battle between the two till Narayana wielded his Sudarshana chakra, the mighty discus. Vrishabhasura believed that since those who were killed by the Lord's discus always attained final moksha or liberation, he too would now achieve it. He requested that the hill be named Vrishabhadri, a boon which Vishnu granted for the Krita yuga.

The sacred hill of Tirumala.
Early 20th century photograph

Seshadri : Once Vayu, the God of the Wind, went to Vishnu's heaven Vaikuntha. As Vishnu was resting with his consort Lakshmi, Adishesha, the divine serpent, was guarding the doorway and refused him entry. The two began to quarrel, till Narayana came out and heard each boasting of his strength and prowess. The Lord suggested a way for them to determine who was more powerful : Adishesha should circle the Ananda mountain and Vayu should try to blow and dislodge him. Several days and nights of furious combat passed by, with neither winning nor yielding, while all the worlds trembled. Finally Brahma and the other Gods told Adishesha that Vishnu and Shiva knew of his strength, so he could loosen his hold and allow Vayu to win. So the serpent loosened his hold and was immediately blown away, with the hill, to the region north of the Swarnamukhi river. As he was very dejected, Brahma assured him that he would be merged with the Venkata hill and Vishnu would reside on him. Then Adishesha fell at Lord Vishnu's feet and was blessed to become the Seshadri range, by which name it was known in the Dvapara yuga. His hood is located at Venkatadri, his body at Ahobalam where Vishnu lived as Narasimha, and his tail at Srisailam where Vishnu was manifested as Mallikarjuna.

Anjanadri : Anjanadevi, the wife of tribal chief Kesari
who lived on the banks of the Pampa river near Hampi,
had no children and consulted Rishi Matanga on what
she should do to conceive. He advised her to go to
the Akasha Ganga stream on the Venkatachala hill and
meditate for twelve years, after which she would
conceive a son. She lived on water for the first year and
on a sweet fruit given to her by Vayu, the God of the
Wind, each day for the next twelve years, till she
gave birth to a son named Anjaneya (later known as
Hanuman), who helped Lord Rama and the Gods.
In honour of Anjanadevi's penance, the hill was named
Anjanadri in the Treta yuga.

When Rama was on his way to Lanka, he was invited to
the hill by Anjana, mother of Hanuman. As he and his
monkey army bathed here before proceeding to Lanka,
their victory over Ravana is attributed to the sacred
Anjanadri hill, according to the Vayu Purana.

Venkatadri : Brahma took a promise from Vishnu that he would redeem the sins of all the pilgrims who came up the hills to the temple. Vishnu agreed, and the Seshadri hills were renamed as Venkata (Vem = dire sins, kata = power of immunity) in the Kali yuga.

The story goes that Madhava, the son of a learned Brahmin named Purandara Somaiyaji, was infatuated by another woman. He abandoned his parents, wife and child and went to live with her till her death twelve years later. Meanwhile, he contracted leprosy and wandered around as a mendicant till, one day, he met a group of pilgrims who were singing in praise of the Lord as they walked on a pilgrimage to Tirumala. Madhava followed them up the hills till he stood in front of the image of Venkateshwara. He realized the enormity of his sin of abandoning his parents, wife and child. Suddenly his body was consumed by flames, the leprosy left him and his body became beautiful once more. So the hill came to be known as Venkatadri, the hill which destroys all sins.

Other names of the hill are

Vaikunthadri, for it was brought from Vishnu's heaven, Vaikuntha;

Simhachala, because it was here that Vishnu took his Narasimha form for killing the demon Hiranyakashipu;

Varahadri, as it was the home of Varaha;

Srisaila, for it was the home of Goddess Sri (Lakshmi);

Anandadri or Kridadri, for it was the site of Vishnu's divine sport;

Pushkaradri, where the red lotus grew in plenty on the hill;

Gnanadri, for it confers knowledge on the devotee;

Chintamani, since it grants the object of one's desire;

Teerthadri, after the many sacred watering spots which are situated here;

Dharmadri, for Dharmadeva, the God of Righteousness who performed penance on the hill;

Kanakadri, where gold and precious stones were once found;

Narayanadri, after a Brahmin named Narayana who did severe penance on the hill and was granted his desire to have the hill named after him;

Nilagiri, for the Vanara chief Nila who once lived here;

Srinivasagiri, where the Lord Vishnu once lived as Srinivasa and married Padmavati;

Garudadri, since it was brought from Vaikuntha by Vishnu's vehicle Garuda.

The Sacred Tank and Holy Waters   Chapter 4

Tirumala hill is a vast area dotted with peaks from which rise lakes and waterfalls. Of these, 108 are believed to be sacred and associated with various epic characters and miracles of Lord Venkatesha.

Swami Pushkarini : The Swami Pushkarini was Vishnu's tank in Vaikuntha, and was brought to the earth by Garuda for Vishnu's use. It is the sacred tank in front of the temple of Tirumala, even regarded as equivalent to the Ganga and other sacred rivers. A dip in the tank cleanses the bather of all sins. The performance of the daily rites or even occasional rites on the banks of the Swami Pushkarini is said to cure deformities of the body and ensure the avoidance of all types of hell. It grants the wishes of those who bathe in it. Like the hill, all the tanks and lakes of Tirumala are sacred and known as "teerthas".

There are seventeen teerthas (holy waters) whose waters are believed to combine in the Swami Pushkarini.

Swami Pushkarini,
the sacred tank of Tirumala

According to the Bhavishya Purana, King Shankhana, a scion of the lunar race, lost his kingdom to Samantha Raja. He therefore left his kingdom and went with his family on a pilgrimage to Sethu in the south and on his return, reached the Swarnamukhi river. He was feeling very sad at having lost his kingdom when a voice directed him to go to Venkatachala, where the Lord is like Kamadhenu, the celestial cow which satisfies all wishes, the Chintamani, the divine stone which grants all prayers and Suradruma, the wish-granting tree. The king was instructed to build his hermitage on the banks of the tank and worship the Lord. The king did as instructed, till one day Lord Vishnu, holding the conch, discus and mace, and flanked by Sridevi and Bhudevi, arose from the Swami Pushkarini on a divine air vehicle. Shankhana praised the Lord and bemoaned the loss of his kingdom. Vishnu blessed him and assured him that whoever bathed in the Swami Pushkarini would get his heart's desire. Shankhana was very happy and started his return journey home. Meanwhile, Shankhana's enemies had been fighting among themselves. The people rose in revolt and threw them out and had set out in search of Shankhana. They met him near the Godavari river and requested him to return and assume his throne. Thus his penance on the banks of the Swami Pushkarini regained King Shankhana his kingdom.

It is believed that the Swami Pushkarini rewards those who bathe in its waters by granting their heart's desire.

Vajra kavacha, a jewelled covering
presented by King Krishnadevaraya

Another story from the Vamana Purana associates Markandeya with this tank. The Rishi Markandeya did severe penance to Lord Brahma who appeared before him. Markandeya asked to be blessed with the opportunity to visit all the sacred teerthas. Brahma replied that it would take a very long time and even Rudra could not undertake and finish such a pilgrimage. However, he added that the reward for bathing in all the holy waters could be obtained from a dip in the Swami Pushkarini on one day in the year — the Mukkoti day — when the waters from all the sacred teerthas merged with the tank. Markandeya did so, and was rewarded accordingly. Other visitors to the Swami Pushkarini were Indra, Chandra, Kubera and the other gods.

Bathing in the Swami Pushkarini is therefore considered to be equivalent to bathing in all the sacred waters.

Rama, son of Dasharatha and an earlier incarnation of Vishnu, visited the hill at the request of Anjana, mother of Hanuman. He and his army, consisting of his brother Lakshmana, his devotee Hanuman, the monkey king Sugriva and the monkey army bathed here, before continuing on their journey to Lanka. They fought and vanquished Ravana, king of Lanka, and his army and Rama returned in triumph to Ayodhya where he was crowned king. The Varaha Purana attributes their success to the bath in the Swami Pushkarini, as it grants success to all those who bathe in it.

Coronation of Rama.
Kalamkari painting from Kalahasti

The Rishi Narayana, after whom the hill was named Narayanadri, bathed regularly in the tank and meditated on its banks.

The Skanda Purana narrates the story of Dharmagupta, the son of king Nanda. One day, Dharmagupta went out on a hunting expedition when it became dark. He decided to stay in the forest when he was chased up a tree by a lion. There he found a boar who had also taken refuge. Dharmagupta and the boar decided that each would stay awake half the night while the other slept. The boar was on the first shift and, as the king slept, did not yield to the lion's entreaties to throw down the sleeping man. Then it was the king's turn to stay awake. As the boar slept and the lion cajoled, the untrustworthy king decided to push down the boar as the lion's prey. But the boar woke up in time, assumed the form of a sage and saved himself by holding on to a branch. Dharmagupta was cursed to become a lunatic. When his retinue saw him, they rushed to king Nanda who took him to Rishi Jaimini for advice and help. The sage, whose divining powers made it possible for him to find out what had happened, advised the king to take his son to the Venkatachala hill and make him bathe in the Swami Pushkarini to rid himself of his sin. The king did so, and Dharmagupta was cured. He returned to rule his kingdom wisely and well.

25

Kapila teertha and waterfall at the foot of the hill

Similarly, the Rishi Kashyapa, who was an expert in curing snake bites, was persuaded by the snake king Takshaka to go back to his village, as a result of which Takshaka bit king Parikshit, who immediately died. He went to his guru, Sakalya Maharishi, who advised him to go to Venkatadri, bathe in the Swami Pushkarini and then worship the Lord. Kashyapa did so, and was absolved of his sins.

The river Saraswati prayed long and hard and, when Vishnu appeared before her, said she wished to be regarded as the most sacred. He told her that while it was not possible for her to be more sacred than the Ganga, she (Saraswati) would reside beside his temple on his hill at Venkatadri in the Swami Pushkarini. Once a year, all the sacred waters, including the Ganga, merge with the Swami Pushkarini to wash off their sins.

The sacred Mukkoti or parva day of the Swami Pushkarini tank takes place on dvadashi (the twelfth day of the waxing moon) in the month of Dhanur (December-January) when Vishnu's chakra or discus is taken in procession and immersed in the Swami Pushkarini, when all the Gods bathe in the tank. A bath at the same time, it is believed, washes away all sins.

There are seventeen sacred lakes — teerthas — whose holy waters mingle with the Swami Pushkarini. They are

Kapila teertha, a sacred pool in front of which sage Kapila worshipped the Linga;

Shakra or Vajra teertha, situated on the hill above the Kapila teertha, where the God Indra (Shakra) was released from the curse of Gautama Rishi;

Vishvaksena saras, where Vishvaksena, the son of Varuna, meditated and became the commander of the divine forces;

Agnikunda teertha, situated above the Panchaayudha teertha, which is inaccessible;

Brahma teertha, that which cleanses great sins (even those such as murder);

Panchaayudha teerthas, five pools named after the five weapons of Vishnu : shankha (conch), chakra (discus), gada (mace), sharanga (bow) and khadga (sword);

Saptarishi teertha, seven water sources named after the seven rishis or sages Kashyapa, Atri, Bharadwaja, Vishwamitra, Gautama, Vashishtha and Jamadagni.

The seventeen teerthas are put into seven groups, each possessing greater merit than the other. A pilgrimage to the sacred teerthas on Venkatadri is equivalent to visiting all the other holy waters. Apart from these, there are many other teerthas on Venkatachala, such as

Akashaganga teertha : Situated to the north of the temple, this is the site where Anjanadevi performed penance for twelve years and Hanuman was born. Every day silver potfulls of water from this teertha are brought by one of the seven families of Acharyas, for the daily ceremonial bath (Abhishekha) of the Lord.

Vaikuntha teertha : Situated in a cave to the north-east of the temple, a few members of Rama's monkey army saw Vishnu's Vaikuntha inside the cave, hence the name.

Sanaka-Sanandhana teertha : Once the home of saints and yogis, it is believed that a dip in this lake will confer yogic powers. A bath in the month of Maargali or Dhanur (December-January) will liberate a person from earthly bondage.

Jabali teertha : This was the site of the hermitage, first of Jabali Rishi and his disciples and, later, of Agastya Rishi and his disciples, and is located two miles to the north of the temple. It is believed to have miraculous powers to relieve bodies possessed of spirits and ghosts.

Pandava teertha : Situated a mile away from the temple, to the north east, it is named after the five Pandava brothers who lived on the Venkatachala hill for a year. At the end of the year, Yudhhishthira dreamed that as they had lived here for a year, they were now absolved of their sins, and would be victorious in the war to regain their kingdom from the Kauravas. Thereafter, the Pandavas left for Hastinapura, and the teertha was named after them.

Papavinasha teertha : A low waterfall three miles from the temple, a bath in its holy water on the seventh or twelfth day of the waxing moon in the month of Ashada (July-August) will wipe out the sins of previous births.

Papavinasha teertha and waterfall

Chakra teertha : To rid the world of the demons who were a menace to life, a devotee named Padmanabha meditated on Lord Venkatesha for twelve long years at this teertha, till the Lord sent his chakra Sudarshana to destroy the demons. Images of Lakshmi — Narasimha and Sudarshana chakra are installed here. On the twelfth day of the waning moon in the month of Kartika, an offering of payasam (sweetened milk and rice pudding) is offered to the images from the main temple, and then distributed to those who bathed in the teertha.

Kumara teertha : An elderly Brahmin lived alone on the hill, meditating on Lord Venkatesha. One day, when he had lost his way, a young boy appeared before him, led him to a lake and asked him to take a dip in the lake. The old man did so, and was transformed into a sixteen year old youth. The young boy revealed himself to be Lord Balaji, blessed the old man and disappeared. From then on, the lake was known as Kumara (youth).

Kumaradhara teertha : In order to absolve himself of the sin of Brahmahatya (killing a Brahmin) when he killed the wicked Tarakasura, Kumara or Kartikeya performed penance at this teertha which was named after him. According to another story, a blind old man with a decrepit body was told by Lord Venkatesha to bathe here. On doing so, he became a youth of sixteen years. In honour of this miracle, the teertha was named Kumaradhara.

Rasayana, **Valighna** and **Jarahara teerthas** are three teerthas not visible to the human eye.

Thotti teertha : Situated in the sanctum sanctorum, the sandal and saffron-mixed abhishekha waters used for the ritual ceremonial bath of the Lord's image are collected on Fridays in this teertha. Drinking these waters will destroy all sins.

Kayarasayana teertha or ashthi saras : Also hidden from view, the waters of this teertha, if drunk, purify the body immediately. Thondaimaan had been entrusted by a Brahmin with the care of his pregnant wife when the latter went on a pilgrimage to Kashi. Unfortunately, the woman died. Venkateshwara instructed Thondaimaan to dip her corpse in this water. He did so, and she came back to life.

Ramakrishna teertha : Six miles to the north of the Venkatesha temple, a person named Krishna excavated this pool. Later, a rishi named Ramakrishna meditated here for centuries till an ant hill grew around him. To test his concentration, Indra sent down thunder, lightening and rains, but Ramakrishna did not budge. But the crest of the anthill broke, and Lord Venkatesha appeared before

him, with the promise that whosoever bathed in the teertha on full moon day would be released of all sins.

Tumba, Tumburu kona : Gandharva Tumburu cursed his lazy wife to become a toad and live in this lake till rishi Agastya arrived at the teertha and described its merit to his students, after bathing in its waters. On hearing his words, she would regain her form. It happened thus, and she became a Gandharva again. The teertha is thus named after the Gandharva Tumburu.

Viraja teertha : The divine Viraja river is supposed to flow under the feet of Lord Venkateshwara. The water is collected in a small tub at the entrance to the temple store room.

Deva teertha : Located in a thick forest to the north-west of the temple, a bath in this teertha on a Thursday combined with the constellation pushya or on a Monday combined with the constellation shravana will destroy all sins and confer longevity and happiness.

Phalguni teertha : Arundhati, wife of the Rishi Vasishtha, meditated on the banks of this lake till Goddess Lakshmi appeared and blessed her with immortality. A bath in this teertha on a full moon day in the month of Phalgun (March-April) will release the bather from the cycle of birth, death and rebirth.

29

Vishnu resting on Ananta-Sesha,
surrounded by his consort Lakshmi,
the personifications of his weapons,
and the Devas, 5th century A.D.,
Gupta; Deogarh, Madhya Pradesh.

Vishnu — Narayana Chapter 5

Balaji or Venkateshwara is a form of Vishnu, the Protector of popular Hinduism, who manifests himself on earth whenever Dharma — righteous duty and good conduct — are in danger.

Shiva destroys evil and Brahma creates life, while Vishnu preserves all that is good. He is the Preserver, the sustenance of all life. Brahma, Vishnu and Shiva form the Trinity of popular Hinduism and, as Creator, Preserver and Destroyer, represent the cycle of birth, life and death.

Vishnu, the all-pervading, the Preserver

The earliest reference to Vishnu is in the Rig Veda, the most ancient and sacred Hindu text which is of divine origin, ageless and eternal. The name Vishnu means all-pervading and reflects his solar nature. He is called an Aditya, or solar deity, or even the sun itself.
He is responsible for the solar year and the seasons.

Vishnu, 8th century A.D., Pallava bronze; Thanjavur, Tamilnadu

Vishnu Trivikrama and his vehicle Garuda, 8th century A.D.; Rajavalochana Temple, Madhya Pradesh

31

Vishnu, 8th century A.D.;
Sultanpur, Uttar Pradesh

*chaturbhih saakam navatim cha naamabhishchakra na vrittam
vyateera veevipat.*

(He, like a rounded wheel, sets in motion his ninety
racing steeds together with the four — Rig Veda, I. 155.6).

His three strides (trivikrama) through the earth,
firmament and heaven represent the three stations of the
morning, evening and midday sun.

*idam vishnurvichakrame tredha nidadha padam
samoolhamasya paamsure.*

(Through all this world strode Vishnu; thrice his foot he
planted. The whole was gathered in his footstep's dust —
Rig Veda, I. 22.17).

The dust raised by his steps envelop the world and is
symbolic of the all-embracing sun's rays. While the first
two places where he keeps his foot — the rising and the
setting sun — are known to man, no mortal can discern
the highest limit.

*paromaatrayaatanvaa vrudhaan na tai mahitvamanvashnuvanti.
ubha te vidam rajasi prithivyaa vishno deva tvam paramasya
vitse.
na te vishno jaayamaano na jaato deva mahimnah
paramantamaap.
udastamnaa naakamrushpam bruhantam daaghartha praacheem
kakubham prithivyaah.*

(Men come not near your majesty who grows beyond all
bound and measure with your body. Both your regions of
the earth, O Vishnu, we know : you, Lord, know the
highest also. None who is born or being born, God
Vishnu, has reached the utmost limit of your grandeur.
The vast high vault of heaven you have supported, and
fixed the eastern pinnacle securely — Rig Veda, VII. 99.1)

*tadasyapriyamabhi paatho ashyaam naro yatra devayavo
madanti.
urukramasya sa hi bandhuritthaa vishnoh pade parame madhva
utsah*

(May I attain to that his well-loved mansion where men
devoted to the gods are happy. For there springs, close
akin to the wide-strider, the well of nectar in Vishnu's
highest footstep — Rig Veda, I. 154.5)

This third step, or Vishnupada, is described by the Katha
Upanishad as the goal of spiritual attainment of the
human soul.

In the Rig Veda, Vishnu, the all-pervading sun, partners
Indra, the god of thunder and rain, to fight Vritra,
the demon of drought, who is finally killed by Indra.
This is the story of the sun and rain wiping
out drought, an eternal Indian preoccupation, and
ushering prosperity.

Vishnu on Adishesha,
6th century A.D., Chalukya;
Badami, Mysore

32

This aspect is reflected in the story of Balaji. The sun is the source of life and sustenance on earth and Vishnu as the all-pervading Aditya preserves life on earth.

The Rig Veda also refers to Vishnu as Girikshit and Girishtha, associating him with the mountains and hills. Again, Vishnu's residence on the Venkatadri hills reflects this aspect.

Finally, Vishnu, in the Veda, is the protector of the sacrifice and, in this form, obtains the earth, the aerial expanse and the sky for the sacrificer. Venkatesha is the beneficial, the giver of boons who is worshipped by his devotees for his munificence.

The Rig Vedic descriptions of Vishnu are important in that they are manifested in various forms in the later incarnations of Vishnu. All the incarnations are of solar lineage. His all-pervading nature makes him manifest himself everywhere, in every age. He is the giver of boons and prosperity, the munificent god, the destroyer of famine, whose home is the life-giving waters themselves. He is the destroyer of evil, who manifests himself on earth whenever Dharma, or the divinely-ordained righteous order, is threatened, and who has taken several incarnations to save the earth and righteousness. He is the final refuge of all human beings.

The images of Vishnu are generally four-armed, holding the conch, discus, mace and lotus, although they may also be two, eight or sixteen-armed, holding the sword and bow and arrow in addition. His vehicle is Garuda the eagle, on whom he often sits, and his couch is Adishesha, the many-hooded serpent. His consorts are Sri (Lakshmi), the Goddess of prosperity and Bhu, Goddess Earth.

It is the all-pervading Lord Vishnu who resides on Venkatadri hill as Venkateshwara, Balaji or Srinivasa, for the benefit of the world.

Narayana as Padmanabha resting on Adishesha, surrounded by the waters. Lakshmi is at his feet, Brahma is seated on a lotus issuing from Vishnu's navel

Vishnu reclining on the cosmic waters on the coils of Adishesha with the lotus of life on which sits Brahma, the Creator, rising out of his navel; Pahari miniature painting

Narayana, the refuge

At the time of the dissolution of the world, following the great flood, there was only water everywhere and the sage Markandeya was wandering, lost, when he met a male child lying on the branch of the nyagrodha (banyan) tree. The child introduced himself as Narayana, the creator and destroyer of the universe, saying,

aapo naaraa iti puraa sangyaakarma krutam mayaa
tena naaraayano apyukto mama tattvayanam sadaa

(Formerly I gave the waters the name nara. Because the waters have always been my abode, I am therefore called Narayana — Mahabharata, III. 189.12952.)

The later Manusamhita, Vishnu Purana and Harivamsha add the information that the waters were called nara because they were the resting place of the Supreme Lord Narayana.

Narayana is represented variously : as Narayana, the refuge of all souls, as Ranganatha, with Sridevi and Bhudevi, and as Vata-patra-shayi, the child lying on the leaf of the *Ficus krishnae* plant. In the first two forms he lies on the many-hooded serpent Adishesha. All these forms are aspects of Vishnu the all-pervading, resting on the waters, the refuge of all souls, the destroyer of evil and saviour of good.

Narayana, as he rests on the eternal waters, becomes the Creator who brings forth life from the ocean. The Rig Veda tells us that "the waters, they received that germ primeval wherein the gods were gathered all together. It rested upon the Unborn's navel, that One wherein abide all things existing".

His creative powers are represented by a lotus issuing out of his navel, bearing Brahma the Creator. Narayana is "older than the oldest ones" and the "Lord of life". And creation comes from the life-giving waters.

As Narayana rests on the waters, there is tranquility on earth. When the world is denuded and barren, or in danger from an evil power, Narayana incarnates himself on earth, first to destroy evil and then to re-create a new and better world order. As the Preserver, he protects the world for the good, for his devotees. Thus he combines in himself the three qualities of Destroyer, Creator and Preserver.

Images of Narayana generally show the God resting on his couch, the many-hooded serpent, Adishesha, holding the conch, discus, lotus and mace. Sometimes a lotus, on which Brahma is seated, is shown coming out of his navel.

Incarnations and Manifestations of Vishnu — Narayana

Although Vishnu has taken several incarnations on earth, as and when Dharma or the divine law was in danger, there are generally ten accepted incarnations corresponding with the various stages of evolution of life on earth. With the exception of Krishna who was a full incarnation of Vishnu, the others were part incarnations who even met with other incarnations or Vishnu himself during their sojourn on earth.

The images of the incarnations may be two, four, eight or sixteen-armed, holding the conch, discus, mace, lotus and sword. Or they may hold none of these, such as Parashurama with the battle-axe or Rama with the bow and arrow or Krishna with the flute.

Matsya, the fish : At the end of the last age or kalpa a great flood devastated and destroyed the world. Vishnu the Preserver commanded Rishi Satyavrata to collect the seven great sages and samples of every animal, bird, plant and seed in a boat. Lord Vishnu then appeared in the form of a gigantic fish and dragged the boat through the turbulent oceans all through the long night of Brahma, till the deluge ended and Brahma created the present world. Thus was born Manu, the progenitor of the human race. This story resembles the tale in the Bible's Book of Genesis, a story which first appeared on the tablets of ancient Babylon and probably goes back to an actual flood which took place in the ancient past, probably in the sixth millennium B.C. Another version is that an evil demon stole the four Vedas and hid them beneath the ocean. Vishnu took the form of a giant fish and retrieved them.

Chapter 6

Vishnu as Matsya; Kondapalli, Andhra Pradesh

Matsya killing Damanaka, the demon who stole the Vedas and hid in a conch-shell; Pahari Painting

Vishnu as Kurma; Kondapalli,
Andhra Pradesh

In the story of evolution, the fish represents the earliest form of life on earth, a form of life which lived under water. In iconography, Matsya is represented with the upper torso of a man and the lower torso of a fish.

Kurma, the tortoise : The wicked demons performed austerities and obtained strengths with which they harassed the Gods and constantly fought with them. The Gods then implored Vishnu to deliver them from this evil. Vishnu advised the Gods to make peace with the demons and unite with them to churn the ocean for amrita, the nectar of immortality. So the Gods lifted the mountain Mandara, used it as a churning rod, and the snake Vasuki as the rope. But the earth sank under this weight. Vishnu assumed the form of a giant tortoise and went beneath the mountain, serving as a base on which the mountain could pivot. When the nectar of immortality was churned, the demons again started fighting for it. Now Vishnu assumed the form of a beautiful woman, Mohini, to distract the demons and give the nectar to the Gods, who now attained immortality. The incident of the churning of the ocean is known as the samudra manthana. This incarnation was extremely popular in South East Asia. The story is beautifully carved in relief on the walls of the temple of Angkor Vat in Cambodia. The entrance to Angkor Thom is made up of five gates consisting of the mountain Mandara crowned by four-faced heads, variously described as Brahma, Vishnu, Shiva and Lokeshvara. However it is obviously Vishnu who appears atop Mandara during the samudra manthana on the beautifully carved reliefs on the walls of both Angkor Vat and Angkor Thom. On either side of the gates unfold the coils of the serpent Vasuki held by larger-than-life demons and Gods churning the ocean in unison.

The tortoise represents the next stage of evolution, the amphibian who could live in and out of water. In iconography, he is generally represented with the upper torso of a man and the lower of a tortoise.

Gods and demons churning the ocean of milk; temple carving

Vishnu as the mighty boar Varaha, raising the earth, goddess Bhudevi, from the ocean floor; Halebid, Karnataka

Varaha, the boar : During the great flood, the earth was submerged under water. The wicked demon Hiranyaksha abducted Goddess Earth — Bhudevi — and took her away under water. So Vishnu took the form of a boar, dived deep into the water, fought and killed the demon and rescued Earth. The rescue of the Earth represents the Supreme saving the world from evil.

This incarnation is generally represented as an enormous boar carrying Goddess Earth in a human form on his tusks. Varaha may be represented in three ways :

Bhu Varaha, holding Goddess Earth — or Bhudevi — seated on his tusks or in his hand or on his lap and holding the blue lotus in her hand.

Adi Varaha, standing with one foot on Adishesha, representing the life-giving waters and carrying Bhudevi holding the blue lotus and seated on his tusks or in his hand or on his lap.

Pralaya Varaha, sitting on a throne which he shares with Goddess Earth holding the blue lotus.

Yagnya Varaha, seated on a throne with Lakshmi and Bhudevi on either side holding the lotus and blue lotus respectively.

Varaha represents the land animal who no longer lives in the waters, an important step in evolutionary history. He is intimately connected with the land which he rescues from the waters.

Vishnu as Varaha, the guardian of the earth-goddess Bhudevi; calendar art

37

Vishnu as Narasimha, the man-lion;
Halebid, Karnataka

Narasimha, the man-lion : Hiranyaksha had a brother
Hiranyakashipu who now began harassing the Gods.
Actually the two were Jaya and Vijaya, the gate-keepers of
heaven, who had incurred the displeasure of Vishnu and
were cursed to be born as demons and Vishnu's
enemies in three births. Hiranyakashipu performed
severe penances and obtained several boons from Brahma
which made him invincible : he could be killed by neither
man nor animal nor weapon, neither inside nor outside
a building, neither in the day nor in the night, neither
on earth nor in the sky. Now Brahma was helpless when
the demon turned against the Gods who, in turn, turned
to Vishnu for help.

Hiranyakashipu's son Prahlada was a devout worshipper
of Vishnu, making Hiranyakashipu very angry. In one
of his fits of anger, Hiranyakashipu asked Prahlada
where Vishnu was and kicked a pillar. And out came
the terrible form of the man-lion Narasimha, neither man
nor animal. Sitting on the doorway, neither inside
nor outside, at dusk, which was neither day nor night,
Narasimha tore apart the wicked demon.

There are three types of Narasimha images :

Sthauna Narasimha, with Hiranyakashipu stretched out on his lap, his belly ripped open by the man-lion;

Girija Narasimha, a Yogic figure sitting on a lotus seat with his legs tied in place by a belt called the yogapatta.

Yanaka Narasimha, sitting either on his vehicle Garuda, the eagle, or on his couch Adishesha, the serpent.

There are several Narasimha shrines in the Eastern Ghats, of which the Venkatachala hill is a part. In fact, he is probably the most important incarnation of Vishnu in this region.

Narasimha represents a transitional stage on the evolutionary ladder, the transition from animal to man.

Narasimha, the man-lion incarnation of Vishnu, whose fury was restrained by his gentle consort Lakshmi; calendar art

Vamana, the dwarf : The roots of the Vamana incarnation are to be found in the Vedic Vishnu who, as Trivikrama, traversed the universe in three steps.

Bali was the grandson of Prahlada. He performed many austerities which won him control over the earth, heavens and the nether regions, all of which he ruled with his demon hosts. Seeing her son Indra lose his heavenly kingdom, Aditi, the mother of the Gods, went to request Vishnu to restore them their kingdom. So Vishnu took the form of a young Brahmin boy, a dwarf, and approached Bali, who was performing a sacrifice. Against the advice of his guru Shukracharya who recognized Vishnu in the dwarf, Bali said he was honoured by Vishnu's presence and offered Vamana whatever he wanted. Vamana asked for the space covered by his three paces, a request which Bali acceded to at once. Immediately, the dwarf became the giant Trivikrama. With his first step he covered the heavens, with the second the earth. As there was no place for the third, Bali offered his head. Pleased with Bali, Vamana allowed him to return to rule the nether worlds with his demons, and the heavens were returned to the Gods.

The artistic representations of this incarnation are of two extremely different forms :

In one, Trivikrama is a gigantic figure with one foot on the ground and the other lifted high across the heads of all the attendant deities. He is generally multi-armed and surrounded by several Gods and holy men.

In the other, Vamana is represented as a short Brahmachari holding an umbrella, water pot and book and wearing a ring made of kusha grass on his third finger.

On the evolutionary scale, Vamana is the early *Homo sapiens,* short in stature and still growing.

Vishnu as Vamana; Kondapalli, Andhra Pradesh

Vishnu as Parashurama; Kondapalli, Andhra Pradesh

Parashurama, with the battle axe : The Kshatriyas (warrior caste), goes the story, had become arrogant and quarrelsome. So the world had to be saved from them.

Vishnu was born as Parashurama, the son of Renuka and Jamadagni, a holy sage. One day, King Kartavirya, while out hunting, visited the hermitage of the sage who entertained the royal entourage with the help of his cow Surabhi who could fulfil any wish. The king asked for the cow, but Jamadagni refused, upon which he was killed by Kartavirya's son. Parashurama learned of this on his return to the hermitage and swore vengeance on the entire Kshatriya race. He first killed Kartavirya and his son. Thereafter, he pursued all Kshatriyas, who trembled at his name and tried, unsuccessfully, to hide themselves from the avenger. Parashurama killed every Kshatriya and wiped out the entire race from this earth. His incarnation came to an end only when he met the next incarnation Rama, after which Parashurama retired to the hills. Images of Parashurama show a man in a deer skin, unshaven, holding a battle-axe.

Parashurama resembles the Neolithic cave man of popular imagination, wielding a battle-axe, representing an age of hand-to-hand warfare. This is also his position on the evolutionary scale.

Rama : Rama was born the son of Dasharatha, the king of Ayodhya. The story of his marriage to Sita, his banishment to the forest by his step-mother for fourteen years, the abduction of Sita by the wicked king Ravana of Lanka, Rama's killing of Ravana, his triumphant return to Ayodhya and coronation as king make up the Ramayana, an epic familiar to every Indian and which forms the basis of Indian social and moral

Rama, Sita, Lakshmana and Hanuman; contemporary illustration.

values. Rama represents perfection, a fountainhead of goodness and justice, upholding his father's promise even when it is unfair to him, faithful to a single wife and a role model for all times.

Images of Rama are invariably a part of a group consisting of Rama holding a bow and arrow, his brother Lakshmana holding the same weapons, Rama's wife Sita and his devotee Hanuman, the monkey faced god, loved by all.

In evolution, Rama is early man as we know him, part of a social order and fulfilling his duties, the provider and protector. His weapon, the bow and arrow also portray the development in weaponry from the hand-to-hand fighting equipment of the previous incarnation.

The coronation of Rama; Thanjavur painting

41

Krishna playing the flute in Vrindavan; North Indian Miniature painting

Krishna : Unlike the other incarnations, Krishna is regarded by his devotees as a full manifestation of Vishnu. Born to Vasudeva and Devaki, he is taken away to the home of the cowherds Nanda and Yashoda by his father to be saved from death at the hands of his uncle Kamsa, king of Mathura, who, it was predicted, would be killed by their eighth child, Krishna. He grows up in Brindavan and the stories of his childhood there make up the legends of the child-god Krishna who kills several demons and his wicked uncle. He is Arjuna's charioteer in the war of Kurukshetra between the Pandavas and the Kauravas, and is the author of the Bhagavat Gita. The story of the Kurukshetra war and of Krishna makes up the great Indian epic, the Mahabharata.

Krishna is represented with his flute in one hand and flanked by his wives Rukmini and Satyabhama, manifestations of Sri (prosperity) and Bhu (earth). He is often represented with the conch, discus and lotus or mace : the first two were obtained by Krishna as he killed the evil demons.

Krishna is the thinking man, the philosopher, statesman and intellectual who plans with his brain rather than fight with his hands. This is the beginning of the evolution of modern man.

Krishna's advice to Arjuna (the Bhagavad Gita)

Buddha : According to the Bhagavata Purana, Vishnu, as Buddha, was born to deceive the enemies of the Gods. Buddha advised the Asuras (demons) to renounce the Vedas, making them lose all their power. Thus the Gods were able to establish their supremacy.

Born Prince Siddhartha, he renounced all his worldly possessions and became a mendicant. He rejected sacrifices and rituals, and taught his devotees to be free of desire, lead a disciplined life and search for the answers to the riddles of the world within oneself. The Buddha is an example of Upanishadic philosophy in action. He is represented sitting in the lotus pose on a lotus seat, blessing the worshipper, after attaining enlightenment.

Buddha is the enlightened man, a step up the ladder of evolution, a man of peace preaching non-violence in preference to war.

Kalki : This incarnation of Vishnu has yet to arrive. In Kali yuga, the present age, people will not follow the Vedas and dharma, foreign barbarians will rule and there will be so much evil that Vishnu will arrive on a white horse to destroy the evil. The world will go up in flames and peace, purity and righteousness will be restored on earth. Kalki is represented either with a horse face or riding a horse.

This is the future of man, destroyed in an apocalypse sent to destroy the earth.

The Buddha; bronze from Nagapattinam, Tamil Nadu

Vishnu as Kalki, the horseman of doom, who dismantles the corrupt world so that it can be reassembled in purity; temple carving, Gujarat

Other Forms of Vishnu :

Vishnu incarnates himself on earth whenever Dharma or the divinely ordained laws and duties are in danger. The number of incarnations varies from text to text, from seven according to the Vishnu Purana to twenty four according to the Bhagavata Purana and twenty six according to the Devi Bhagavatam. However, ten is the most popular and frequently-used number and the incarnations are invariably known as the Dashavatara (ten incarnations) of Lord Vishnu.

Although Vishnu has ten official incarnations on the evolutionary scale, he manifests himself from time to time in various other forms. **Venkateshwara** is one such form. Some of the others are

Balarama, the brother of Krishna, who is regarded by some as the incarnation in place of the Buddha. Others regard him to be an incarnation of Adishesha. He is represented by the plough;

Dhanvantari, the father of Indian medical systems, particularly Ayurveda;

Hamsa, the mythical wise swan;

Hayagriva, a horse-headed human figure, regarded as the God of learning;

Vishnu as Balarama, the lord of farmers bearing a plough; Mysore painting (left) and as Hayagriva, the horse-headed Vishnu, sometimes mentioned in the list of avataras; Mysore painting (right)

44

Dattatreya; contemporary illustration

Dattatreya, a representation of Vishnu as the Trinity, with the three heads of Brahma, Vishnu and Shiva, and accompanied by four dogs representing the four Vedas, and the sacred cow;

Jagannatha, Lord of the Universe, a common name for Vishnu and a form which is sanctified in the temple at Puri, along with his brother Balarama and sister Subhadra;

Jagannatha with Balarama and Subhadra; wood carving, Orissa

45

Vishnu and Lakshmi on Garuda the eagle, the vehicle of Vishnu (right) and Vishnu as Mohini (below); Halebid, Karnataka

Lakshmi- Narayana, a composite figure of Vishnu seated with Goddess Lakshmi on his lap, the merging of the male and female principles;

Mohini, the form of a beautiful woman assumed by Vishnu to distract the asuras or demons from the amrita, the nectar of immortality;

Varadaraja, the giver of boons, whose most famous temple is the Varadaraja Perumal temple of Kanchipuram in Tamilnadu;

Padmanabha, the lotus-navelled One, a reference to Narayana lying on the ocean with the lotus issuing out of his navel. Brahma sits on the lotus, signifying the beginning of all creation;

46

Ranganatha; contemporary soapstone
carving, Pondicherry

Ranganatha, or Vishnu resting on his great serpent
couch Adishesha, with Sridevi and Bhudevi at his feet.
He is represented thus at Srirangam near Tiruchi,
where the great Vaishnava philosopher Ramanuja spent
most of his life;

Vitthala, a form of Krishna accompanied by Rukmini,
the deity of the temple of the same name at Pandharpur
in Maharashtra.

Stone-carved image of Vitthala;
Pandharpur, Maharashtra

47

Vaikunthanatha in bronze at the Hari Rai Temple, Chamba, Himachal Pradesh

Vaikunthanatha, combining the heads of a man, woman, lion (Narasimha) and boar (Varaha), a form popular in the early medieval art of Kashmir, and the Himalayan region;

Shreenathji, a form of Lord Krishna originally installed by his grandson Vajranabha in ancient Vraja on the Yamuna and later reinstalled in Nathdwara during the period of Muslim vandalism;

There are many more, impossible to list fully. Nearly every temple of Vishnu, Shiva and Shakti has a local name or manifestation of the deity, running into several million forms of the Supreme Being.

In the Bhagavat Gita or the Song Celestial, Vishnu, as the divine incarnation Krishna who is performing the role of the charioteer of Arjuna, tells the latter that whenever Dharma, the divine code of moral and religious duty, is in danger, he will be reborn again and again, in many different forms. Apart from the main incarnations, Vishnu has manifested himself time and again, whenever Dharma was in danger, and will be manifested many more times in the future, as the world of human beings plunges into greater evil and chaos.

Shreenathji, a form of Lord Krishna, Gujarat; contemporary illustration

Origin, History and Administration of the Temple

Chapter 7

Origin of Balaji — Venkateshwara

Who was Venkateshwara? Today the devotee accepts him unquestioningly as a manifestation of Lord Vishnu, but his identity has been a subject of bitter debate for centuries. The origins of the God are shrouded in a mystery which will probably never be solved. We can only discuss some of the theories.

The name Venkateshwara

The name Venkata is exclusive to the Lord of the hill. It does not appear anywhere else, either in literature or in religion, it is not used for any other deity anywhere, except in recent temples built to replicate the Lord of Tirumala. Venkata has two differing meanings, according to Sanskrit texts :

The first is "Destroyer of sins". The Brahmanda and Bhavishyottara Puranas, both medieval Sanskrit works, say that "vem" means dire sins and "kata" is the immuning power. Brahma took a promise from Vishnu that he would redeem the sins of all the pilgrims who came up the hills to the temple. Vishnu agreed, and the Seshadri hill was renamed as Venkata. Thus Vishnu came to be known as Venkateshwara or Lord of Venkata.

The second meaning, according to the Vayu Purana, another medieval work, is "giver of worldly wealth". "Vem" is derived from amrita or nectar and "kata" from aishwarya or affluence, says the Purana. This meaning relates more to the God's qualities than to the actual etymology of the word.

The etymological roots of the word are hard to find in Sanskrit. The nearest words in Sanskrit are "vyamah kata" which mean "enveloping different kinds of sins" and the earliest appearance of the name is in medieval Puranic literature, after the 10th century A.D.

On the other hand, the word Venkatam, describing the hill, first appears in the Tamil grammar Tholkaappiyam, belonging to the pre-Christian era (about 200 B.C.). Venkadam means "burning debts" ("ven" = burning and "kadan" = debts), a reference to Venkatesha's loan from Kubera. Another meaning in Tamil is "burning mountain slopes" ("kadam" also means a mountain slope), a meaning with interesting anthropological connotations. The latter could either refer to the forest fires, which used to be very frequent (and which are still a problem on these dry deciduous hills), or to the act of clearing the forests, an important event in local history which was

Venkateshwara, the Lord of the hills

carried out by Thondaimaan, who is closely involved with the legends of Venkatesha and is credited with the construction of the temple.

In popular perception in South India, Venkatesha is collecting money to pay off his debts. Pilgrims flock to Tirumala to pour money into the hundi, in the hope that he will reward them in return. The branches of the banks situated in the Tirumala hills probably receive the largest daily collections of money in the whole country, from the amounts deposited by the devotees in the hundi or given by them for the performance of various rituals and special offerings.

However, the name Venkata still remains a mystery. Venkateshwara is the Lord (Ishwara) of Venkata.

Skanda? Shakti? Shiva? Vishnu?

The biggest mystery of all is which God could he be — Skanda, Shakti, Shiva, Vishnu, all or none? This has consumed scholars and been the subject of bitter debate for centuries.

50   Balaji smeared with sandalwood paste and turmeric

Hindu deities are generally identified by their attributes, vehicles and distinguishing marks. Venkatesha has no attributes. The original stone image has a crescent mark on the forehead and holds nothing, the jeweled conch and discus being later detachable additions. There are some distinctly Shaivite features such as the hair, which consists of matted locks (jata·juta), the God's snake-shaped ornaments and the cobra slung over his right arm.

Skanda

In the Tamil tradition, Skanda or Kumara is the God of the hills and nearly all his temples are situated on at least a hillock. Also, there are frequent references in early Tamil literature to festivals on the Venkadam hill, including the hunting festival. Kumara is the God of the hunters and hill festivals are conducted in his honour all over South India. Further, the sacred tank or teertha is named the Swami Pushkarini, Swami being an appelate of Skanda (Kumaraswami). But Swami could also mean God in general. Finally, his attributes, described above, are also undoubtedly Shaivite in nature. He is the son of Shiva.

Shakti

Another view is that it is a form of Durga or another Shakti. The drapery of the Lord resembles a sari. The ceremonial bath (abhisheka) is performed only on Fridays, the day of the auspicious bath (mangala snana) for women, with sandal paste and turmeric, both women's cosmetics, to the chanting of the Shri (Lakshmi) Sukta. The Thomala Seva is also known as Bhagavati aradhana. Above, on the vimana of the temple, crouches Devi's symbol, the lion. The Devi Bhagavatam describes the Lord of Tirumala as Shri Venkateshwari, the only deity for Kali yuga. And finally, according to North Indian tradition, he is known as Balaji, derived from "Bala" the Universal Mother, a woman's name.

Shiva

The Shaivites maintain that the matted hair, the cobra on one arm, the snake ornaments and the crescent on the head are undoubtedly marks of Shiva. Significantly, the pooja is done with the leaves of the bilva (Bengal quince or *Aegle marmelos*) tree : bilva leaves are used only in Shiva temples, never in those of Vishnu. The earliest Tamil Vaishnava saints — Poygai Alvar, Bhutat Alvar and Pey Alvar who lived between A.D. 500 and 650 — as well as Nammalvar, regarded as the most important and the greatest of them all, have conceded that the deity is both Shiva and Vishnu, an admission they would not have made if there was no trace of Shiva in the Lord of Tirumala. Finally, the Purusha Sukta and Shri Sukta are

51

recited by Smarthas (Dikshitas or Aiyars), just as it is a Smartha who performs the sacred abhishekha for the main deity on Fridays. The Vaishnavas recite the Tamil Divyaprabandham, the passion songs of the Alvars who sang of their divine Lord.

Vishnu

The Silappadikaaram (8th century A.D.) refers to the deity as Vishnu. The author, a Jaina who would not have been concerned with the rival claims of the various sects, says, "Lord Vishnu… is seen in a standing posture on the top of Vengadam hill…adorned with a brilliant cloth of gold round his loins and…a beautiful garland on his chest and (he) holds in his lotus-like hands the invincible discus and milky white conch". The later Alvars have referred to the deity as a manifestation of Vishnu in their songs. The Brahmanda, Bhavishyottara and Vayu Puranas describe Venkatesha as a manifestation of Vishnu.

The arguments for identifying the God exclusively with Vishnu were first made by the Vaishnava philosopher and missionary Ramanuja, who lived between 1017 and 1137 A.D., and who is credited with the establishment of the temple as a Vaishnava shrine. Ramanuja is believed to have participated in a great debate over whether the image was of Shiva or Vishnu.

The Yadava king, who was a Vaishnava himself, ruled in Ramanuja's favour. Thereafter, Ramanuja reconsecrated the image as a manifestation of Vishnu. While there is no historical evidence for this, it seems fairly certain that the cult of Venkatesha as a manifestation of Vishnu gained prominence at this time.

The Verdict

The arguments for and against each identification have been going on for over a thousand years, if not more. There is no clear answer, except some likely inferences.

The discovery by Thondaimaan, while ascending the hill with a hunter, of a half-buried image "standing under a tree, with the lower part of the body hidden in an anthill", as well as the references in literature to unspecified but famous festivals in the hills, suggest a folk or tribal origin for the deity. Even today, there are several ambivalent images of deities all over India who are identified with either Shiva or Vishnu but are actually neither, nor any of their subsidiaries, and who combine within them male and female, Hari (Vishnu) and Hara (Shiva). Also, Hindu deities generally carry some attribute — the original stone image, it is believed, carries none.

The answer probably lies in the work of the earliest Vaishnava saints who saw both Shiva and Vishnu in their

Lord, even though they were diehard Vaishnavas.
Poygai Alvar says

"His name is Aran (Hara or Shiva) and Naranan (Narayana)
His vehicle is the bull (Nandi) and the bird (Garuda)
His word is the book and marai
His residence is the hills (Kailasa) and in the waters
His function is destruction and protection
His weapon is the trident and the disc
His form, though One, is fire and dark cloud."

Can there be a more beautiful description of the Oneness
of Shiva and Vishnu?

Nammalvar, 16th century bronze, Tamilnadu

Pey Alvar sings

"He has in his form the flowing matted locks and the high peaked crown
The shining dagger and the disc
The snake coiling around him and the golden string around his waist
In him, my father on Tirumalai,
The two forms have gracefully blended into One".

Bhutat Alvar also visualises the Lord as a combination of Shiva and Vishnu, while Nammalvar, writing in the 8th century, concedes that Vishnu, as the Lord of Tirumala, has merged in himself Rudra, Brahma and Lakshmi, accepting all three forms of the Supreme.

The attempt to identify him exclusively as Vishnu and deny the Oneness of the various forms of the Lord took place only during the period of Ramanuja, who is well-known for his missionary zeal to convert temples, Gods and people to Vaishnavism. As Ramanuja had the support of his rulers, the Yadava kings, and their successors, the powerful Vijayanagara emperors who were worshippers of Vishnu, the Lord of Tirumala became irrevocably identified with Vishnu.

In Balaji — Venkatesha, the devotee sees his personal God, be it Shiva or Vishnu, Skanda or Shakti. There can be no greater proof of the Universal Nature of the Lord than that he combines within himself the main deities of Hinduism.

Ramanuja, founder of the Vishishtadvaita school of Vaishnava philosophy; stone carving, Tirumala Temple

Origin of the stone image

Our sources of information about the hill temple range from literature to oral traditions to epigraphs. The earliest reference to the hill is by the Tamil grammarian Tholkaappiar in the second century B.C. who refers to the hill as the northern boundary of the Tamil world :

vada vengada then kumari yaayida thamil kurum nal ulaham

(the tract between vengadam in the north and (Kanya) Kumari in the south is said to be the good world of the Tamils).

The next references are in Tamil Sangam literature. Poet Maamoolanar refers to the Vengadam hills in the second century A.D. The Ahanaanooru mentions Pulli, chieftan of the region around Vengadam, the narrow passage across the hill which one had to cross to come out of Pulli's territory and the festivals for which Vengadam was famous. Nakkirar and Kanakkanayanaar are two Shaivite saints who refer to Vengadam, the latter also mentioning the hosts of elephants in the forests.

Although none of these writers speak of the God of Vengadam, the references to Thondaimaan, the name of the hills — Venkatadri — which is associated with the destruction of sin, and the festivals for which the place was famous make it very likely that the God was known by 200 B.C. itself.

The first actual reference to a deity appears in the Silappadikaaram, a Jaina epic of the 8th century A.D. which defines Vengadam as one of the three Vaishnava temples. The author says that "Lord Vishnu of the lotus eyes is seen in a standing posture on the top of Vengadam hill which is full of waterfalls and where the effulgent rays of the sun and the moon fall on the image. The Lord is adorned with a brilliant cloth of gold round his loins and he wears a beautiful garland on his chest and holds in his lotus-like hands the invincible discus and milky white conch. He looks like a black cloud with a streak of lightning and a rainbow". What is interesting about this stanza is the author's assertion that the sun and the moon shone on the image, indicating that it either stood out in the open or under a tree (which was and still is very common) or under an open-sided pavilion. Obviously, no temple had been built as yet.

The statue is, visually, pre- or early Pallava, the identification coming from its style and attribute-less state (it is believed that the original stone figure does not hold any weapons, these were added much later by Ramanuja). It is also likely that there was an earlier image made of a perishable material like wood or clay.

The tradition of an image of worship, as described in Tamil literature, is much older than the present stone

Utsava murti of Balaji — Venkatesha decorated with pearls

figure which, at the earliest, belongs to about the sixth century. When stone sculpture became popular in the South, many of the earlier wooden or terracotta figures were replaced. The Vishnu temple of Varadaraja Perumal at Kanchipuram is one such example where the original figure made of fig wood has been preserved in the temple tank and is taken out only every twelve years, while the main deity under worship, today, is made of granite.

Songs of the Alvars

The Vaishnava saints of Tamilnadu — the Alvars — have sung extensively about the Lord of Vengadam. Ten out of twelve Alvars visited Tirumala and composed songs in his praise. The first three — Poygai Alvar, Bhutat Alvar and Pey Alvar — lived in the early years of the eighth century and sang of the Lord of Vengadam. The Thiruvaimoli of Nammalvar, who lived in 798 A.D. and is considered to be the greatest of the Alvars, contains several stanzas describing the God. While the existence of the temple is not known, the hill was held in high esteem as the annihilator of sins. In 1803, the then Collector of Chittoor, G. Stratton notes that "In such veneration is even the hill held that pilgrims resorting to the pagoda prostrate themselves to the ground (on) first getting a sight of the range of hills connected with it."

56   A Vaishnava Alvar or saint

The Alvars also describe the thick jungles, interspersed with streams and waterfalls, surrounding the hills which abounded with elephants, snakes, monkeys and boars, and where the Korava tribes lived. In fact the later Yadava rulers of the region are known to have originally belonged to the Kurumba tribe who overthrew the Vedars and Ventari hunting tribes of the hills. In 1804, the existence of Yanadis "who collected honey and bees' wax and sandalwood, fruits and roots" is mentioned.

Kamban, the author of the Tamil Ramayana, refers to Vengadam as a sacred hill where holy men live, who do good deeds without any thought of reward and who have attained a state of bliss.

There are several references to the Venkata hill in medieval Sanskrit literature, as the earlier references from the Puranas testify. Telugu and Kannada literature are also replete with references to the God, indicating his widespread worship.

The Puranas ascribe the construction of the temple to Thondaimaan, the ruler of Narayanavanam, who discovered the image of the God "standing under a tree, with the lower part of the body hidden in an ant-hill" when he ascended the hill with a local hunter, and who constructed the prakara and gopuram, maybe even the original temple complex. Although Thondaimaan's role in the Venkatesha legend is obviously exaggerated, he was actually a historical figure who probably lived around 550 A.D., the pre-Pallava period to which the style of the main stone statue corresponds. He is reputed to have cleared the jungles around Kalahasti and established the kingdom of Thondaimandalam. The region between the Vengadam hills and as far south as Chidambaram is known as Thondaimandalam even today. There are some villages around Tirupati which still bear traces of Thondaimaan, such as Thondamaanaadu and Thondavaada. He is described as the illegitimate son of Kulottunga Chola of Thanjavur and was probably related to the Pallavas, who were also known as the "Thondaiyars"or "Kattu Vettigal", meaning "those who cleared the forests", an appropriate appellate for Thondaimaan. According to the Tamil text Perumpanatruppadai, the Pallavas are so-called because their ancestor Vishnu came floating on the leaf ("pallava" means leaf) of a "thondai" creeper, and that is why the name Thondaimandalam was given to their kingdom.

Recorded history

While the origin of the image is shrouded in the mists of time, the temple has a far more certain history. The recorded history of the temple begins in the small village of Tiruchanur, once known as Tiruchchokinur, where there is an inscription regarding the gift of a perpetual

Thondaimaan, Pallava ruler of Thondaimandalam which included Tirumala-Tirupati

Krishnadevaraya, Vijayanagara
emperor, Tirumala temple

light to the hill God Tiruvengadattu Peruman Adigal by Vijayaditya, a local ruler of the Bana dynasty who lived between 830 and 850 A.D. An inscription dated 970 A.D. on the north wall of the hill shrine records the gift of a silver image (now placed in the Tiruvilankovil), a necklace and other ornaments and lands in Tiruchanur by Samavai, daughter of a Pallava chieftan and wife of a Kadava chief. In 1000 A.D., we are told, the wife of the Chola king Parantaka II presented a gift of a gold plate studded with precious stones to Venkateshwara. There are several subsequent records of grants made in the Chola and subsequent Pandya periods.

But it was the Yadava Rayas, Chola feudatories of the region between 1184 and 1355, who contributed greatly to the development of the temple. They gifted several lands, villages, cows, ornaments and images to the temple. It was during their rule that Ramanujacharya established the temple as a Vaishnava shrine. Ramanuja visited the area two or three times. The first occasion was when he lived at the foothills for a year, to study the Ramayana from his maternal uncle Tirumalai Nambi. The second occasion was as the leader of the Sri Vaishnava community of Srirangam. The third occasion was in his old age.

In 1303, Allauddin Khilji tried to invade Andhra desha, but was repelled. In 1309 he sent his general Malik Kafur on a military expedition to the south. Malik Kafur ravaged the kingdoms of the Kakatiyas, Hoysalas and Pandyas, plundered and took away their wealth and destroyed their temples.

In the Koil Alagu, the history of the famous temple of Srirangam at Tiruchirapalli (Trichi), it is said that on hearing of the approach of Malik Kafur, the local people who were celebrating the annual festival took some urgent measures to save the deity from destruction by the Muslim general. They walled up the sanctum sanctorum which housed the main deity, hid the jewels and smuggled the bronze processional image away to Tirumala which, fortunately, was too inaccessible for Malik Kafur.

The Tirumala-Tirupati region was taken over by the Vijayanagara empire, founded in 1336 A.D. by Harihara and Bukka of the Sangama dynasty, two brothers who were inspired by their philosopher friend and guide, Saint Vidyaranya, to establish a kingdom to protect the religion and culture of the Hindus. An important event of this dynasty was the return of the processional image to Srirangam. Devaraya II of the Sangama dynasty was devoted to the Lord and made several benefactions.

The Sangamas were followed by the Saluva, Tuluva and Aravidu dynasties of the Vijayanagara empire, all of whom were great devotees of Lord Venkateshwara. The temple structure evolved in this period. Saluva Narasimha

Raya endowed the village of Durgasamudram in 1482 A.D. for the purpose of constructing gopurams (gateways) in Tirumalai and gave several gifts to the temple. But the greatest patronage was received during the reign of Krishnadeva Raya of the Tuluva dynasty, who visited the temple on all important occasions, and his brother Achyuta Raya. The two kings and their queens made costly gifts of gold, jewels and lands, and instituted and supported several festivals.

The rule of the Aravidu, the last dynasty, was one of constant war, culminating in the ultimate destruction of the capital Vijayanagara (modern Hampi) and the empire. From 1650 to 1800 the Tirumalai–Tirupati region was ruled by the Muslims — as the Sultans of Golconda and the Nawabs of Carnatic — who extracted tribute and taxes from the temples.

The management of the temple was in the hands of the Sthaanathaar, the traditional managers, and there is no record of any fees being collected from the pilgrims. In 1724, Asaf Jah, Nizam of Hyderabad, appointed Daud Khan as the Nawab of the Carnatic. The latter demanded an annual tribute of rupees two lakhs to leave the temple alone. To make up this amount, several levies were introduced which the pilgrims had to pay, fees for reciting the mantras, tonsuring the head, lighting camphor, attending the archana, presenting a cloth, offering a food item and so on. In 1753, Muhammad Kamal marched towards Tirupati to plunder the temple, so the British sent a detachment to ward off the attack. Thereafter, the British took over the revenues of the temple, away from the Nawab.

The revenues passed to the East India Company in 1801, who continued the practice. In 1843 the Company handed over the temples to the mahants (priests) who managed them till the Government of the erstwhile Madras Presidency took them over in 1933 and put them under the management of a Board of Trustees.

Two well-known English officials who were devotees of the temple, although as non-Hindus they were never permitted to enter, were Sir Thomas Munroe and Lord Williams. The former suffered from an acute and incurable stomach pain. He was advised by a devotee of Lord Venkatesha to take a vow that he would visit Tirumalai and worship Lord Venkatesha if he was cured. Sir Thomas agreed and was cured. He visited Tirumala, although he was not permitted to enter the temple, and created an endowment for a daily offering of a gangalam (a huge vessel) of pongal (a rice and lentil dish), and gifted the village of Kotavayulu in Chittoor district for this purpose. His gift is still known as Munroe gangalam. Similarly, Lord Williams, who was cured of an incurable chronic illness, instituted the Lord Williams chali pandili

Sir Thomas Munroe, Governor of Madras and devotee of Balaji, statue at Chennai

59

(drinking water service) at Mokalametta, along the footpath to Tirumala, a charity continued even today.

With the formation of the state of Andhra Pradesh, the control and management of the temples passed on to the new state. Today the Tirumala Tirupati Devasthanam manages Tirumala and all the associated temples. The revenue goes to maintain the properties, staff and the many charities and educational institutions of the Devasthanam.

Administration and facilities at Tirumala-Tirupati

The Tirumala Tirupati Devasthanam (TTD) is administered by a Board of Trustees appointed by the Government of Andhra Pradesh. The administration is carried out by the Executive Officer, generally an I.A.S. officer, although the legendary Dr. C. Anna Rao, who held the position for several years and was responsible for many of the present facilities for pilgrims, did not belong to the cadre. The administration can be divided into two sections — general administration and temple administration — the former managing the Devasthanam's properties, finance and staff, and the latter involving the maintenance of the temple and facilities for pilgrims. The main offices of the Devasthanam are at Tirupati, with camp offices on the hill and information

Vaikuntham queue complex;
Tirumala

centres in various parts of India. The average annual income is about Rs. 300 crores, most of the money coming from hundi offerings.

Accommodation is available for all purses, from free choultries for the poor to cottages for families and air conditioned suites for the very rich. A lot of money is spent on providing civic amenities in Tirumala and Tirupati, for widening and maintaining roads and supplying water to the town of Tirupati, including the construction of a canal from Srikalahasti to Tirupati in order to bring the Telugu Ganga water to the temple town. Free bus facilities are available from the railway station to the top of the hill. The Devasthanam also provides several services such as religious propogation, education, afforestation, medical facilities and succour for the poor and disabled.

Free food is provided to the devotees, with an average of 30,000 people fed every day. The Sri Venkateshwara Nithya Annadanam Trust makes it possible for the devotee to contribute his mite to this scheme.

The Dharma Prachara Parishad promotes religious knowledge among young people, propogates the basic ideals of Hinduism and runs two Veda pathashalas at Tirumala and Hyderabad. The Devasthanam runs five institutions for Sanskrit and Vedic learning, four colleges, two for the Fine Arts, a new training centre for sculpture, one polytechnic, one Ayurvedic college, one institute for Yoga and allied sciences and ten schools in Tirupati and elsewhere in Andhra Pradesh. The Publications Department and Press bring out several publications about the temple and religious tenets, as well as regular journals. The Oriental Manuscripts Library is a storehouse of manuscripts. Two Museums — the Hall of Antiquities at Tirumala and the Sri Venkateshwara Museum of Temple Art at Tirupati — provide a feast of art. Several kalyana mandapams (wedding halls) have been constructed or are under construction — 170 in Andhra Pradesh, 3 in Karnataka, and 1 each in Kerala (at Guruvayoor, a famous temple town), Orissa and Tamilnadu — which are made available at very low rates or even free of charge.

3025 hectares of land covering the slopes of the hill have been afforested and restored to their original biodiversity by the TTD's Forest Department. The Garden Department has developed beautiful ornamental and flower gardens on 455 acres of land on the hilltop. The Sri Venkateshwara Vanaabhivriddhi Scheme provides several opportunities, through the Vriksha Samvardhanam, Vriksha Prasadam, Smaraka Vanuly and Vana Samrakshana Bhagaswayam schemes, for the public to participate in the Devasthanam's afforestation programmes and earn great merit.

Hundi, early 20th century
photograph

The Devasthanam runs the Ashwini Hospital at Tirumala and the TTD Central Hospital at Tirupati, besides several clinics and dispensaries to provide free medical aid to the pilgrims. A speciality hospital — Sri Venkateshwara Institute of Medical Sciences — has made advanced technology available for diagnosis and treatment for the poor. Philanthropists wishing to contribute for health services can donate to the Sri Balaji Arogyavaraprasadini Scheme.

Several facilities have been provided for the disadvantaged. The Sri Venkateshwara Poor Home is the largest asylum in the country for leprosy patients. There is a Venkateshwara School for the Deaf and a Technical cum Production Centre for the Handicapped. The Balaji Institute for Research and Rehabilitation of the Disabled (BIRRD) provides advanced surgical techniques for poor and needy orthopaedic patients free of cost, while the Artificial Limb Fitting Centre provides aids and appliances for the poor free of cost. The Venkateshwara Balamandir is an orphanage established in 1943, while the Sri Venkateshwara Karunadhanam is a home for beggars.

Every pilgrim who visits Tirumala and puts money in the hundi or collection box can be satisfied that he is contributing to helping the poor and the needy, the young and the handicapped. This is one place where the Lord answers the prayers of all his devotees.

62 Venkateshwara carved out of sandalwood; Karnataka

Images of Lord Venkateshwara and Other Deities

Venkateshwara : His image is regarded as a swayam vyakta murti, or one which is self-manifested. He is an "eka beralaya", where only one form of God receives all the worship.

Carved out of black granite, Balaji stands on a high lotus pedestal. The image is about nine feet tall from the base of the pedestal to the tip of the crown. Every Friday the deity is given a ceremonial bath (abhishekha), when he is visible without his jewels or the huge Vaishnava caste mark on his forehead. His eyes look directly at the devotee and he smiles with an expression of inner tranquility and outer happiness. His crown or makuta, also sculpted in stone as a part of the image, is over twenty inches high. His flowing hair or jata juta is curled and rests on his shoulders.

The image is four-armed : two arms at the back are held up and curled into fists, ready to hold weapons. The conch and discus are attached separately. The front right hand is in the varada mudra (boon-giving hand posture), while the front left hand rests lightly on the hip in the katya vilambita hasta indicating that the Lord protects and blesses his true devotees. A seated Lakshmi is carved on the right side of his chest. The sacred thread (yagnyopavita), four necklaces, a thick girdle around the waist, snake-shaped armlets and a pair of anklets adorn the figure. On his shoulders are marks resembling the scars made from carrying a bow. The deity is a typical image of the Pallava or pre-Pallava period.

Chapter 8

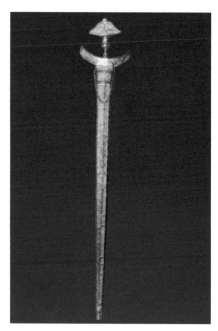

Gold surya kathari or sword

Gold waist band sculpted with the ten Avataras

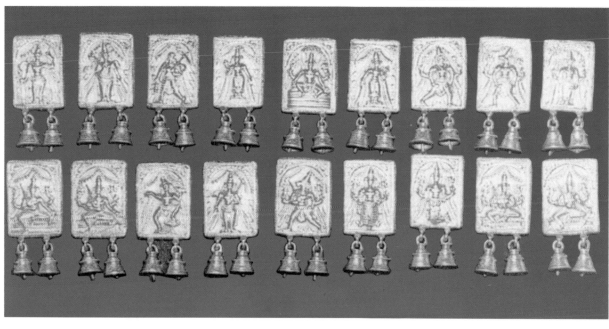

GOLD JEWELLERY

1. Crown 2. Bhuja kirti or shoulder plate
3. Chakra 4. Kavacha or covering 5. Snake armlet

DIAMOND JEWELLERY

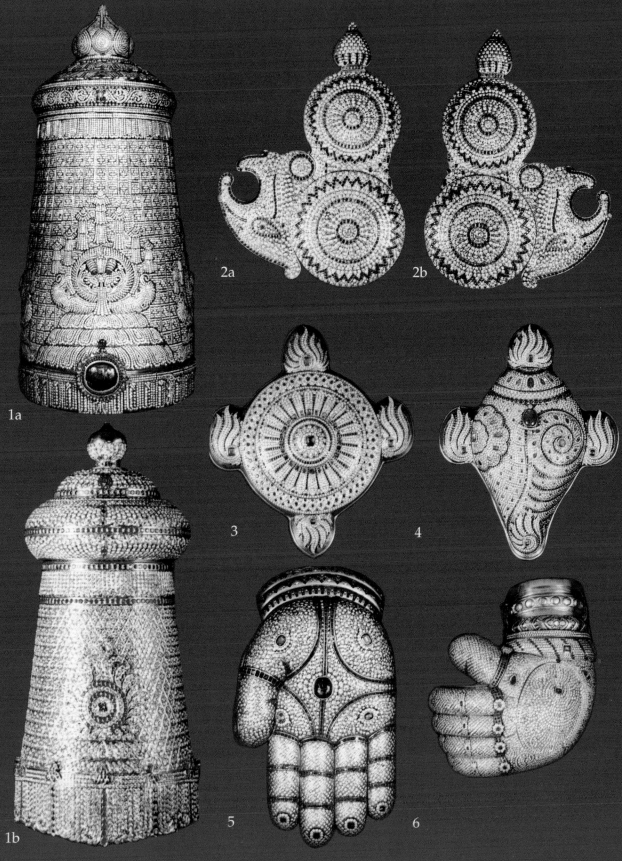

1a,b Crown or Kirita   2a,b Makara kundala or Makara shaped earrings right and left
3. Chakra   4. Shankha   5. Right hand covering in varada hasta
6. Left hand covering in katya vilambita hasta

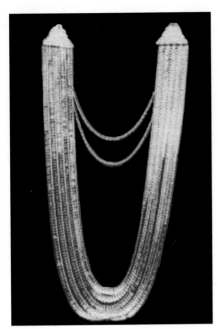

Gold necklace engraved with the thousand names of Venkatesha

Ornamentation : Balaji is covered with a gold plate which replicates, in elaborate detail, the carvings on the stone. His crown, conch, discus, his two hands (in the varada and katya vilambita pose) and various other ornaments are studded with diamonds and other precious stones.

There are certain unique pieces. He is decorated with an emerald 3-inches in diameter called the "meru pacha", which is said to be the world's largest. His gem-studded gold crown is believed to be a gift of Akasha Raja. His gold earrings are crocodile-shaped makara kundalas. One of his necklaces consists of a pair of gold-encased tiger claws, the other is a garland with the image of Goddess Lakshmi carved out on each pendant. He wears a necklace consisting of saligramas mounted in gold and engraved with the Sahasranama, the thousand names of Vishnu, and another necklace of tulasi seeds. His armlets are shaped like two hooded cobras. Venkatesha's sword is known as the suryakatari and hangs from his belt, which is decorated with the ten avataras or incarnations. Truly, his ornaments are unique and wonderful.

On his chest, Venkateshwara bears two sculptured plaques of gold: the four-armed lotus-bearing Goddess Lakshmi seated on a lotus adorns the right side, while Padmavati adorns the left.

The image of Balaji is wonderful and awesome. It inspires intense devotion and faith, love and veneration.

Bhoga Srinivasa, silver image,
66   Pallava, A.D. 970

Other images in the garba griha

Bhoga Srinivasa : In A.D. 966, the Pallava queen Samavai gifted a silver image of Bhoga Srinivasa, along with considerable lands and jewellery, to the temple, and an inscription on the north wall records this gift. Bhoga Srinivasa is a replica of the main deity. Whereas the ceremonial bath for the main deity takes place only on Fridays, the Bhoga Srinivasa murti is bathed every morning during the abhishekha and put to sleep during the ekanta seva in a silver cradle every night for eleven months, signifying that the Lord is the immortal child of creation. The image is always kept in the garba griha (sanctum sanctorum).

Krishna : In the month of Dhanus (December-January), Krishna receives the honour of the ekanta seva instead of Bhoga Srinivasa. Krishna is depicted as a dancing child with a ball of butter in one hand and the other stretched out during the dance. This iconographic form is known as the Navaneetha Nritya, and the God is accompanied by his consort Rukmini, an incarnation of Lakshmi. No separate rituals are conducted for Krishna who merely shares the daily offering to Lord Venkatesha.

Pearl pandal for Kaliya Mardana Krishna

67

Utsava murti : This is a three foot high processional image made of panchaloha bronze, a replica of the main stone image, but with the chakra and conch on the two upper arms. Sridevi and Bhudevi flank him on the right and left. The Goddesses are two-armed, one arm in the kataka hasta, with the finger tips loosely joined to form a ring in which a fresh flower can be inserted daily, and the other in the gajakarna (elephant ear) hasta, stretched out away from the figure. The image is mentioned in an inscription dating to A.D. 1339. The deity is also known as Sri Malayappa Swami or Malai Kuniya Ninran Perumal, meaning "the One who stood on the hill which bowed very low", a reference to the popular legend of the image's discovery in a mountain glade.

Venkateshwara with Sridevi and Bhudevi — bronze utsava murtis

Koluvu Srinivasa : Every day, after the tomala seva, koluvu or durbar is held in the Tirumamani mandapa. The image is then brought out of the sanctum and seated on a silver chair with a gold umbrella above. The idol officiates for the main deity during this function, when the day's astrological predictions and the previous day's accounts are read out. The image is also known as Bali Beram. Surrounded by a simha toranam, he is seated on a silver chair and canopied by a golden umbrella as he listens to the almanac and the accounts.

Ugra Srinivasa : Originally known as Venkatathuraivar, this idol represents the God in anger. It is taken out only thrice a year, on uttama ekadashi, mukkoti dwadashi and dwadasha aradhana, before dawn, and is hurriedly returned to the sanctum before sunrise. The sun's rays must not touch the image; if it does, it is said that the world will come to an end.

Rama, Sita, Lakshmana and Hanuman : These four copper icons were probably installed in the twelfth century by Ramanujacharya, according to the Shri Venkatachala Itihasa Mala. According to a legend associated with the Rama incarnation, Ravana had actually abducted Vedavati, the Maya (illusion) Sita. So Sita, who was an incarnation of Lakshmi, had taken a promise that the Lord would marry Vedavati in a future incarnation. Padmavati was Vedavati reborn. In celebration of this legend, the four copper images are kept in the garba griha.

Chakrathalvar or Sudarshana Chakra : The personification of Lord Vishnu's discus, Sudarshana is also installed in the sanctum and precedes the Utsava Murti in processions. On Ratha Saptami day, Chakrathalvar has the ritual bath in the Swami Pushkarini.

Angada, Hanuman, Vishwaksena, Ananta and Garuda : These are beautiful copper images exhibited outside the Antarala Mandapam on the Ramar medai (platform).

The metal images are all utsava murtis. During the various festivals in Tirumala, they are decked up in rich jewellery and silks and taken out in procession through the streets, along with the images of Balaji, Sridevi and Bhudevi. The various characters are involved with one or more of the incarnations or manifestations of Vishnu.

Angada

Adishesha

Vishwaksena

Tirumala hill with the temple complex in the centre

Gold-plated Ananda Nilaya Vimana of the Tirumala temple

Gold-plated Dhvajastambha of the Tirumala temple

The Temples of Tirumala, Tirupati and Tiruchanur

The Temple of Venkatesha on Tirumala

The temple is a rectangle about 129 by 82 metres, covering an area of about two acres. The whole temple town of Tirumala or Venkatadri is designed and constructed around the temple, an elaborate complex whose every part is utilized for the various rituals and festivals for which Tirumala is famous.

Almost all the sculptures of the temple belong to the 15th, 16th, and 17th centuries, the period of Vijayanagara rule and thereafter. The few remnants of the Yadava period (12th century) at Tirumala include the garba griha and the entrance gopura (gateway). Only the main deity goes back in time to the 6th century.

The Vijayanagara kings and their Nayaka successors were prolific temple builders and renovators. They also favoured very baroque designs and ancilliary structures. The various sub-structures such as the many mandapas were built over high plinths decorated with horizontal bands of animal, plant and floral carvings. The pillars are strikingly tall and monolithic, sculpted with typical Vijayanagara motifs such as warriors, soldiers on rearing horses and rearing yalis (mythical lions), with contrasting geometric shapes and crowned by the four-branched floral volute capitals.

Shankha nidhi at the main entrance   71

Mukha dwaram, the main entrance to the temple

Mukha Dwaram : This is the only entrance to the temple. Facing east, it is surmounted by the Padikavali gopura superstructure and was probably constructed in the 12th-13th centuries. Shankha nidhi and Padma nidhi, the personifications of Vishnu's attributes, flank the entrance.

Sampangi Pradakshina : The path of circumambulation between the two prakaras, it contains several mandapas of architectural and sculptural beauty, as well as the rooms for storing jaggery, the theppam (float festival) items and distributing prasadam, the hall known as the Ramanuja koodam where food is distributed freely to all pilgrims, the Padipotu, presided over by Vakulamalika and where sweets and fried foods are prepared to be offered to Balaji, and the Yamanothurai where the flower garlands are strung for the Lord. Four small mandapas at the corners, constructed by Saluva Narasimha for seating the utsava murtis and offering naivedya or sacred food to the deity for free distribution later to the pilgrims, are held up by pillars and pillarets. The mandapas are no longer in use today. It is likely that there were originally champaka trees in this prakara (champaka=sampangi), giving it the name sampangi, but there are no trees left today.

Vakulamalika who presides over the kitchen or Padipotu

Dancers on the cornice above the Ranga mandapa

Ranganayakula (or Ranga) Mandapa : This is a small pillared hall inside the main gopura. The mandapa has a portico on either side, each containing two rows of four pillars each. The outer pillars are plain while the inner pillars have brackets consisting of a man riding a mythical lion standing on its hind legs on a makara (crocodile), while the cornice above is surmounted by sculptures depicting dancers and scenes from Vaishnava mythology. The mandapa is so named because the processional image from Srirangam (near Trichi) was brought here during the period of Malik Kafur's invasion, and was kept inside a small shrine, now always kept closed.

Ranga mandapa

Venkatapati Raya

Pratima Mandapa : Adjacent to the Ranganayakula mandapa, it contains the several metal statues of the kings of Vijayanagara. The statue of King Venkatapati Raya is five feet high, made of copper and beautifully ornamented. The statue of King Achyuta Raya is 64 inches high and elaborately ornamented, while the 54-inch statue of his queen Varadaraji Amma has been described as the most graceful and beautiful statue in the temple. Achyuta Raya visited the temple three times, first in 1533 when he performed the rituals himself to the chanting of the sahasranama by the priests. He and his queen gifted several villages and ornaments to the temple and instituted new festivals.

The best statues are, however, those of King Krishnadeva Raya and his two queens, Chinna Devi and Tirumala Devi. The king is bare-chested, a tall and warrior-like

King Krishnadeva Raya, Chinna Devi and Tirumala Devi, 16th century A.D. Vijayanagara copper statues

74

figure. The two queens are elaborately-ornamented, in the Vijayanagara style, slim and very beautiful. Krishnadeva Raya, who ruled between A.D. 1509 and 1530, was a devout worshipper of Lord Venkateshwara and visited the temple at least seven times. His literary work Amuktamalyada is dedicated to the Lord. He gifted a crown set with the nine sacred gems (navaratna) and countless other stones, twenty-five silver plates and several villages. Vijayanagara reached the zenith of its power and glory during the reign of Krishnadeva Raya. Numerous temples all over south India were the beneficiaries.

Pillar capital, Tirumala Raya mandapa

Tirumala Raya Mandapa : Also known as the Oonjal (swing) mandapa, it is a long mandapa (108 ft. by 40 ft.) adjoining the Ranga mandapa, consisting of an elevated southern portion and a lower northern portion. The former was built by Saluva Narasimha in the mid-fifteenth century for the Dola mahotsava, or swing festival, and renovated by Tirumalaraja in the sixteenth century. The Utsava murti is brought to this mandapa every day during the Brahmotsava. It has a unique four- pillared mini mandapa in the centre where each pillar is made up of four pillars each, with one six-inch square main pillar and three sixteen-sided minor pillars. On the pillars are carved warriors, some attended by umbrella bearers, riding horses which are standing up on their hind legs over lions. The minor pillars, which stand on lions, make musical sounds when struck, a popular architectural feature of this period. The bas-relief is decorated with carvings of Narasimha killing Hiranyakashipu, Lakshmi Narasimha blessing Prahlada, Srinivasa, Krishna dancing on the snake Kaliya, Vishnu and Lakshmi, Vishnu on Garuda and Rama holding the bow.

On the main pillars of the main mandapa are riders on lions which are standing on elephants. The pillars have some unique sculptures, such as a scene of a man consoling his wife, Krishna enthralling the cows with his flute, Krishna stealing the clothes of the Gopikas (cowherdesses), and so on.

This mandapa also houses the statues of three unknown donors, Lala Khamaram or Thodar Malla, his mother Mohana De and his wife Pitha Bibi.

Lala Khamaram, a donor, with his mother and wife

The Pratima, Ranga and Tirumala Raya mandapas precede the inner gate which takes the devotee towards the main sanctum.

Oonjal mandapam, the hall of the swing

Phoola Baavi : This is the Well of Flowers, a step-well used for disposing used flowers and flower garlands, a practice initiated by Ramanujacharya in the twelfth century, according to the Venkatachala Itihasa Mala.

Aina Mahal : The hall of mirrors of late origin, it is a room, about thirty seven and a half feet by forty three feet, fully lined with huge mirrors. When illuminated, it is a wonderful sight.

Dhvajastambha Mandapa : Also within the Sampangi pradakshina, this is the second mandapa after entering through the main entrance. It gets its name from the flagpole or the dhvajastambha located beside the balipitha, the platform for offerings. It is a tall, circular, wooden pole covered with gilded copper sheets standing on a stone base also covered with gilded copper sheets. Miniature carvings of Krishna — the child dancing in the navaneeta nritya pose, lifting Mount Govardhan and others — as well as Garuda, Hanuman, the discus, etc. decorate the flag pole.

There are some beautiful sculptures on the pillars of this mandapa. A unique four-armed Trimurti holding a conch and discus and seated on a bird, either a swan or a peacock. Other figures include Hanuman, Vishnu and Yoga Narasimha, Krishna and the gopis and Hanuman carrying Mount Sanjeevi. There are also several mithuna figures.

The shankha, Vishnu's conch, on the Dhvajastambha

Gold relief work of Krishna raising Govardhana hill and Garuda on the Dhvajastambha

Inner Gopura : Separating the sampangi pradakshina from the next, the vimana pradakshina, this gopura was probably built between A.D. 1160 and 1170. At the entrance are two bas-reliefs, one showing Venkatesha playing dice with his devotee Hathiram, and the other Rama, King of Ayodhya, with Sita seated beside him, Lakshmana, Bharata and Hanuman paying obeisance and other minor characters of the court.

Vimana Pradakshina : This circumambulatory path separates the inner prakara from the main shrine. Several rooms and mandapas are located here also.

Varadaraja Shrine : This is a small shrine, 20 feet by 15 feet, with an inscription in Tamil of A.D. 1388, containing a standing image. Although the figure is known as Varadaraja, two hands hold the conch and the discus and the other two are in the abhaya (blessing) and katya vilambita (hand on waist) hastas, not the varada (boon-giving). According to local tradition, the image of Varadaraja was brought here from Kanchipuram during the Muslim raids, as was that of Ranganatha from Srirangam, Tiruchirapalli in Tamil Nadu, hence the name Varadaraja.

Kalyana Mandapa : This is a very important hall built in the sixteenth century to celebrate the wedding (kalyana utsava) of Venkateshwara with Sridevi and Bhudevi. Measuring 80 feet by 36 feet, it contains twenty nine pillars, a small platform on the western corner raised on four polished pillars and a small shrine.

The mandapa has some unique bas-reliefs, such as that of a six-armed Vishnu riding Garuda, a rare dancing Vishnu, Narasimha killing Hiranyakashipu, Trivikrama with his right arm and leg raised to the skies with king Bali below, a sixteen-armed personified Sudarshana Chakra, Krishna dancing, and dancing again on Kaliya, Vishnu with his two consorts, Vishnu with Lakshmi, Rama, Krishna with his consorts Rukmini and Satyabhama, other figures such

Varadaraja, Tirumala

77

Venkateshwara with Sridevi and Bhudevi during the Brahmotsavam

Venkateshwara with Sridevi and Bhudevi — bronze
utsava murtis

Krishna, Rukmini and Satyabhama beneath a
golden kalpa vriksha or tree of life

Ramanuja, Tirumala (left) and
Yoga Narasimha, Tirumala (right)

as mithunas, warriors riding lions borne by elephants, and
the inevitable musical pillars of the Vijayanagara period.

The kalyana utsava is also performed in the mandapam in
the corridor adjoining the Phoola Baavi or Well of Flowers
described earlier. Decorated extensively with sculptures of
Lord Vishnu and his incarnations, it is also utilised for
seating the utsava murtis during the Brahmotsavam.

Ramanuja Shrine : Probably constructed in the twelfth
or thirteenth centuries, the installation of the statue is
mentioned in the Venkatachala Itihasa Mala. As the
founder and exponent of the Vishishtadvaita school
of philosophy, his image is found in many Vaishnava
temples. Although no worship is performed for him,
Ramanuja is honoured at Tirumala for establishing the
deity as a manifestation of Vishnu and for establishing the
rituals to be followed.

Yoga Narasimha Shrine : Also known as Alagiya Singar,
Narasimha receives offerings made to Venkatesha in
this shrine which adjoins that of Ramanuja.

The main building houses the Tirumamani mandapa, the
Tiruvilankovil and the garba griha, or sanctum sanctorum.

Tirumamani Mandapa : This mandapa is situated right in
front of the Nadimi padikaavali or the silver doorway of
the inner gopura. Built in the fifteenth century, it is
actually an open, sixteen-pillared hall, now enclosed by
railings. The pillars contain some rare sculptures, such as
Vishnu seated on an elephant, Sita giving her ring to
Hanuman to be taken to Rama, Pattabhi Rama (Rama on
the throne), Rama with the bow, Tara requesting her
husband Vali not to fight Rama, Varaha and Lakshmi,
Ugra (angry) Narasimha emerging from the pillar,
Krishna, Vishnu and many more. The suprabhatam is
sung here every morning, to wake up Venkateshwara.

Nadimi padikaavali, silver doorway
leading to the Tirumamani mandapa   79

Gold relief of Ranganatha,
Tirumamani mandapa (top), and the
huge bells of the Tirumamani
mandapa (right)

The Tirumamani Mandapa also contains the Garuda
shrine, the tall hundi where the devotees place their
offerings and two huge bells. On the outer wall of this
mandapa, facing the inner gopura gateway (or Nadimi
padikaavali), is a gilted carving of Ranganatha, Lord
Vishnu in the shayana or resting position.

Garuda Shrine : Built in the early sixteenth century,
this shrine within the mandapa houses a five feet high
image of Garuda, the eagle vehicle (vahana) of
Lord Vishnu. With outspread wings, Garuda faces
Lord Venkateshwara in worship.

Bangaru Vakili : This is a door of gold, flanked by Jaya and Vijaya, the gatekeepers of Vaikuntha or Vishnu's heaven, constructed in copper. Situated at the back of the mandapam, it contains the manifestations of Vishnu according to the Vaikhanasa Agama sect — Para (supreme form), Vyuha (as creator, protector and destroyer), Vibhava (such as the incarnations), Antaryamin (in the hearts of his devotees) and Archa (tangible and accessible to his devotees).

Bangaru vakili or golden doorway leading into the garba griha

Tiruvilankoyil or Snapana Mandapa : The inscription of Samavai of A.D. 966 mentions that the silver image of Bhoga Srinivasa was consecrated in this mandapa. However, it was subsequently renovated and sculptured pillars added. The bas-reliefs include scenes of Vishnu and his incarnations.

Ramar Medai : Originally a part of the incomplete Mukkoti Pradakshina, it was built in the thirteenth century and is composed of two small platforms holding figures of Hanuman, Angada, Adishesha, Garuda and Vishwaksena, and a two feet high figure holding a light. Medai is a Tamil word meaning platform and denotes the platform which holds the various bronzes and copper icons. These images are taken out in procession during the various festivals.

Sculpture of Rama, Lakshmana and Hanuman on the Snapana mandapa

81

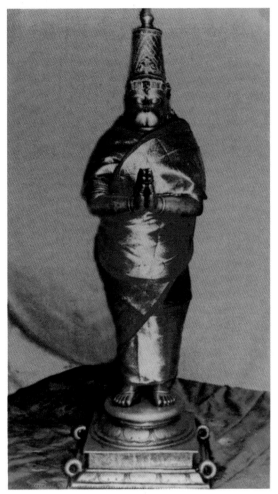

Hanuman, bronze (top) and
Sugriva, bronze (right)

Mukkoti Pradakshina : This is an unfinished
circumambulatory path around three sides — north, south
and west — of the Garba Griha, and is open only on
Vaikuntha Ekadashi day. A small shrine for Vishwaksena,
the divine financial controller, is situated on the northern
side, as is a cement tank which holds the abhishekham
waters. It bears, on its walls, sculptures of columns
growing out of poornakumbhas or cornucopias.

Shayana Mandapa : A small room about 32 metres
square, the 1000 year old image of Bhoga Srinivasa is put
to sleep every night during the Ekanta Sevai.

Garba Griha : Separated from the Shayana mandapa
by the Kulashekhara padi, a step in honour of
Kulashekhara Alvar, a devotee of Vishnu, this is a room
about 13 square metres in area made up of two sets
of walls with an air space between them. It is the
holiest of holies, the sanctum sanctorum which houses
the image of Vishnu as Venkateshwara or Balaji,
the Creator, Preserver and Destroyer.

The temple of Venkateshwara on Tirumala is the only
Eka Murti temple for Vishnu in India, unique in
its origin and situation.

82   An outer view of the garba griha

Artist's impression of Balaji —
Venkateshwara deep inside
the garba griha

The architectural style of a garba griha preceded by a
mandapa and surrounded by a circumambulatory path
came into existence in the eighth century, during the
Pallava period, and the structural temples at Kanchi are
excellent examples of this style. But Venkateshwara
has been standing on the Vengadam hill for over two
thousand years old. The image was obviously housed in
another — even temporary — structure earlier. Or, as the
Silappadikaram says, set where the sun and the moon
shone on it, out on the open hill, beneath a tamarind tree.

Carvings on the outer wall of the
garba griha

Ananda Nilaya Vimana : The tower over the garba griha is given this name. It is a three-storeyed structure with a base 8.5 metres square, and 11.5 high. It has three storeys, the first two rectangular and the topmost circular in shape. There are very few carvings on the first tier and about forty on the second, which includes the Vimana Venkatesha, a replica of the image in the sanctum. The third tier has about twenty bas-reliefs crowned with a huge lotus.

According to the Bhavishyottara Purana, the vimana was first constructed by Thondaimaan. However, as the present garba griha is in the style of the eighth century, the present tower could not have been any earlier.

The tower was first gilded during the reign of Veera Narasingadeva Yadava Raya who ruled between 1205 and 1262 A.D. It was repeated by Saluva Mangideva in 1359, Madhavadasa in 1417 (when he also constructed the Tirumamani mandapa), Krishnadeva Raya in 1518, Koti Kanyakadanam Thathacharya in 1630 and Ramalakshmanadasa in 1908. By 1958 the vimana was completely rebuilt and re-gilted with 12,000 tolas of gold.

Ananda nilaya vimana means abode of happiness. The first view of the vimana, as one climbs the Tirumala tower, is itself an achievement of unity with the Supreme.

The other temples managed by and related to the temple of Balaji are the temples of Varaha, Tiruvilankovil, Padmavathi and Govindaraja.

Ananda nilaya vimana, the gold plated dome of the temple

Varaha temple, Tirumala (left) and
the sacred yantra in the temple (top)

Varaha Temple : Situated in Tirumala, on the west bank
and to the north west of Swami Pushkarini, the temple of
Varaha is believed to be even older than that of Lord
Balaji, for Varaha was the first God on the hill. The pooja
for Varaha should precede that for Venkatesha and the
Naivedyam is sent to him first. After the bell at the
Varaha temple is struck, signifying that the Naivedyam
has reached, the bells at the Venkatesha temple are struck,
and the Naivedyam takes place simultaneously in both
the temples. The God Varaha is known as Gnanabiran,
the giver of knowledge.

However, there is no inscriptional evidence for the
existence of this temple before 1380. Even thereafter, there
are not many references to this temple. Its importance lies
in the sole fact that Tirumala is called a Varaha kshetra.

The image of Varaha inside the
Varaha temple, Tirumala

85

The tank and gopuram (gateway) of the Padmavati Devi temple at Tiruchanur

Tiruchanur

Four kilometers south of Tirupati, on the banks of the river Swarnamukhi, the village of Tiruchanur, formerly Tiruchukanur, existed in Pallava and Chola times, with a village sabha (council) which also managed the temple of Tirumala. There was a Vaishnava community here by the ninth century. At the end of the ninth century, the Cholas conquered ancient Thondaimandalam, of which Tiruchanur was a part. They built the Parasareshvara temple which grew in popularity till the reign of the Vaishnava Yadava Rayas in the thirteenth century. Vaishnavism returned to the region and the temple of Padmavati was built towards the end of the seventeenth century.

Tiruvilankovil : This is the most ancient of the temples of Tiruchanur. According to an inscription of A.D. 826, the Vaishnava community of Tiruchukanur constructed the Tiruvilankovil and consecrated a "proxy" image of Venkateshwara, obviously for those pilgrims who could not manage the arduous trek up the hill. Several gifts to the temple are mentioned in subsequent periods, and the temple reached the zenith of its popularity in the Vijayanagara period. However, the temple is lost today. As most of the inscriptions recording its existence were found either in the Vahana mandapa or on the slabs of the Padikaavali (entrance) gopura of the Padmavati Devi temple, it must have existed within its precincts. The varying styles of the pillars of the Padmavati Devi temple are probably left over from the old Tiruvilankovil and reused.

Padmavati Devi Temple : While Goddess Alarmelmangai Nachiyar (Lakshmi or Shridevi) resides on the right chest of Lord Venkatesha, Goddess Padmavati is never mentioned in the inscriptions of either Tirumala, Tirupati or Tiruchanur. The temple of Padmavati at Tiruchanur consists of a garba griha and an antarala made up of a pillared verandah on three sides and the mukha mandapa on the fourth. The pillars are in the Vijayanagara style. The open mandapa in front contains eight pillars of the Chola period. The vimana is decorated with four lions at four corners and a double lotus containing a gilded kalasha on top. The temple of Padmavati Devi has obviously grown in importance only very recently.

The Goddess Padmavati is seated inside the garba griha with a lotus in each of her two upper hands, her lower hands in the abhaya (do not fear or blessing) and varada (boon giving) hastas. It is said that to achieve the fruits of a pilgrimage to Tirupati, the pilgrim must visit the temple of Padmavati, another aspect of Lakshmi, the Goddess of prosperity.

Gold-plated vimana of the Padmavati Devi temple, Tiruchanur

Govindaraja temple complex with its
many gopurams (gateways),
Tirupati

Tirupati

Govindaraja Temple : The enmity between the Shaivas
and Vaishnavas reached its zenith during the lifetime of
the Vaishnava philosopher Ramanuja. In 1130, Ramanuja
had to find a place to install the image of Govindaraja
from the temple of Chidambaram (in Tamilnadu). He
chose the shrine of Parthasarathi at the foot of the
Tirumala hill. Access to Tirumala was difficult because of
the eleven-mile walk across the hills. The pilgrim could
thus visit the temple of Govindaraja, bathe in the Alvar
teertham at the foot of the hill, and then climb the hill
to visit the shrine of Venkateshwara in Tirupati.

The shrine for Govindaraja came up at the foot of the hill
in the village of Kottur, which was re-named Tirupati by
Ramanuja. It was attached to the shrine of Parthasarathi
and has no separate gopuram. In 1224, Ramanuja and his
uncle Tirumalai Nambi were honoured in a shrine
adjoining the Govindaraja shrine.

It was not easy to develop Tirupati, a small village with
no perennial water source. Ramanuja therefore made it
obligatory for everybody connected with the Tirumala
temple — the priests and their families, the temple
servants and the suppliers of provisions — to live and
own property in Tirupati. However, the Govindaraja

Temple never had enough of an income to be independent and feed its pilgrims. In 1234, the management of the temple was taken over by the managers of the Tirumala temple. With the efforts of Saluva Narasinga Deva and a few private individuals, various parts of the temple were built between 1387 and 1467, but royal patronage came to the temple in fits and starts thereafter. The town of Tirupati grew much later, with the increase of the pilgrim traffic to Tirumala.

Tirupati, at the foot of Tirumala hill, is well-connected to all the southern cities — Chennai (Madras), Hyderabad, Bangalore, Chitoor and Vijayawada. It is an important centre of trade and politics, but it is most famous as the base for a visit to the Balaji temple on Tirumala hill. Most pilgrims tend to say that the temple of Balaji is situated in Tirupati, without realising that Tirumala on the hill is a separate temple town.

Govindaraja with Sridevi and Bhudevi

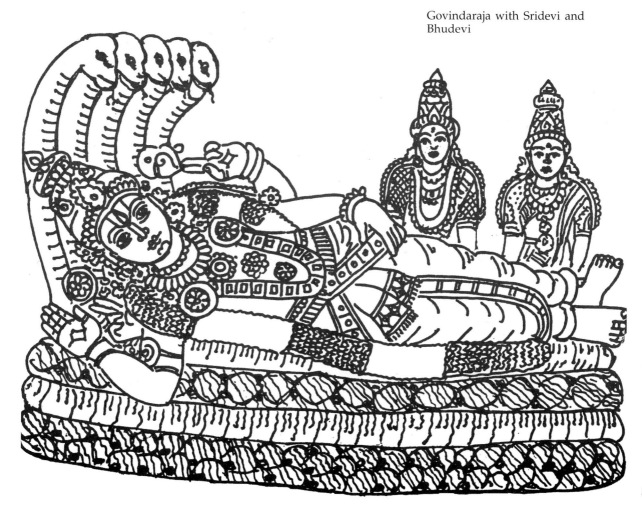

89

Gold Sesha (snake) Vahana

Garuda (eagle) Vahana

Surya Prabha (sun) Vahana

Rama carried by Hanuman

Hamsa (swan) Vahana

Simha (lion) Vahana

Gaja (elephant) Vahana

Ashva (horse) Vahana

Worship of utsava murtis

Decoration of utsava murtis

92   Utsava murtis on the swing

Ratha utsavam

Rituals and Offerings

The Sri Venkatachala Itihasa Mala describes the daily, weekly and annual rituals performed for Balaji, as well as the essential decoration of the main murti. These continue to be followed today.

The face of the image is covered by a huge patch of refined camphor, with the Vaishnava naamam (sectarian mark) over it. 1½ tolas of refined camphor are also used to cover the chin everyday. Katuka or collyrium is applied to the eyes. On Thursdays, all the ornaments are removed to make way for flowers, which form his only ornamentation. On Friday morning, the flowers are removed, the Vaishnava mark is drawn with white earth and the murti receives a full ritual bath (Abhisheka or Thirumanjanam) with turmeric paste. On other days, the daily ritual bath is performed over the gold covers of the main deity, as well as for Bhoga Srinivasa, the utsava murti.

The image is dressed in a long silk or cotton gold lace-bordered cloth known as the Sesha vastram. Along with the sandalwood on his feet, a fresh piece of silk, the Sripada vastram, is used to cover his feet every day, after the Thomala seva. These are given to a devotee.

As the hill is sacred, only those who are in the employment of the temple can live on the hill. In the case of a death, the body is removed to the plains, as cremation is not permitted on the hill. Jivahimsa (killing of any living form) and non-vegetarian food are not permitted on the hill. The temple also has strict rules prohibiting alcohol on the hill.

Visitors caught disobeying any of these rules may be sent away from Tirumala.

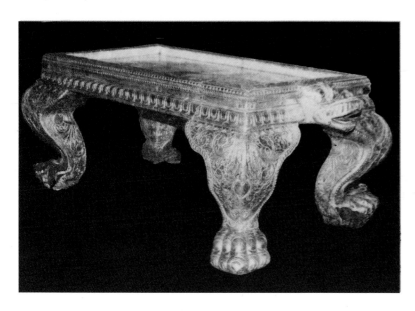

Snapana pitha — the gold platform which holds the utsava murtis

Kalyana katta — the tonsure hall

A unique practice at Tirumala is the tonsure ceremony, when pilgrims offer their hair to Balaji. It is not known when and how this practice commenced, but it has been recorded by an English District Collector in 1831. Many families offer their child's first tonsure to the temple, but many adult men and women also tonsure their hair as an offering or in redemption of a vow. The hair being a symbol of beauty and vanity, removing it and offering it to the Lord are an indication that the devotee is shorn of all vestiges of pride and places himself unreservedly at the feet of the Lord.

The daily poojas are performed according to the Vaikhanasa Agama, initiated by Vaikhanasa rishi. These are :

Balaji, Sridevi, Bhudevi — bronze
94 utsava murtis

Suprabhatam – literally, "good morning", the awakening of the Lord (at about 3 a.m.), when the Bhoga Srinivasa murti laid to rest overnight in the Shayana mandapa is shifted to the garba griha. Navaneeta aarati is performed with cow's milk, butter and sugar, which is then given to the devotees present. All visitors are given the teertha or sacred water which is believed to have been worshipped by Brahma and the devas overnight. The suprabhatam, which consists of the suprabhatam, stotram, prapatti and mangalam, is followed by sankirtanas sung by a descendant of Talapakkam Annamacharya;

Thomala seva – decorating the image with flower garlands, following the cleaning of the temple. Thomala comes from the Tamil word "thodutta malai" or "garland of strung flowers". Water from the Akasha Ganga is brought by a member of the Tirumala Nambi family;

Koluvu or Durbar – the image of Koluvu Srinivasa is kept in the Tirumamani mandapa while the previous day's revenue receipts and the current and next day's almanac predictions are read out;

Sahasranama archana – the recitation of the 1008 names of Venkatesha;

Kalyana utsavam – the wedding ceremony of Venkatesha with Sridevi and Bhudevi. Beginning with the Panchamurti Pooja according to the Vaikhanasa rites, the Mangalya Sutra Dharana is done according to Vedic rites and the three images exchange garlands. The donor of the celebration is given a gift of a cloth and a coin.

Naivedyam – cooked food is presented to Venkatesha behind the closed doors of the Bangaru vakili, after it is presented to Varaha. Thereafter, all pilgrims visiting the hill are entitled to receive free food as 'prasad'.

The temple is famous for its sweet ladoos, and people wait in long queues to buy them.

The gold ritual vessels

Balaji, Sridevi and Bhudevi on the swing (dola)

Saattumurai – the recitation of the Divya Prabandhams of the Tamil Vaishnava saints, the Alvars;

Madhyayana pooja – the recitation of the ashtottara naamaavali — the 108 names of Venkatesha. Naivedyam is offered again;

Dolotsavam – the daily swinging of the icon, performed inside the Aina Mahal;

Sahasra deepalankara – the lighting of the thousand oil lamps outside the temple premises;

Ratri pooja – the recitation of night prayers;

Ardhajama pooja – the offering of sweets before Bhoga Srinivasa is put to bed;

Ekanta seva – a velvet bed is spread on the swing and sweets, milk and fruits are offered, to the accompaniment of music, to Bhoga Srinivasamurti before he is left to sleep for a short night's rest. In the month of Dhanus, the image of Krishna is substituted.

The temple is then closed for the night.

Weekly sevas and utsavas include

Vishesha Pooja – conducted at 6 a.m. on Mondays;

Ashtadala pada padmaradhana seva – 108 golden lotuses are placed at the feet of Balaji, to the accompaniment of Vedic chanting, at 5.30 a.m. on Tuesdays;

Sahasra Kalashabhishekham – the bathing of the deity with a thousand pots of water to the chanting of Vedic hymns on Wednesdays;

Thiruppavada – the special naivedyam offered at 5.30 a.m. on Thursdays;

Poolangi Seva – also performed on Thursdays, when the God is decorated with flowers;

Abhishekham – the ritual bath, performed for the main deity only on Fridays at 3.30 a.m., to the chanting of the Purusha Sukta of the Rig Veda, the Mantra Pushpa shlokas proclaiming that the worship of all Gods reaches Shriman Narayana and the singing of the Nachchiyar Prabandam in Tamil.;

Vastraalankara seva – a set of new clothes are presented to the God on Fridays.

The Vengadam hill has been famous, since time immemorial, for its festivals. This tradition continues even today. Only those festivals still current are mentioned here. The most important festivals are the annual celebrations.

Dhvajaarohanam – the raising of the flag

Brahmotsavam : The origin of this festival has been described in chapter 2. While one Brahmotsavam was conducted initially, in A.D. 966 the Pallava queen Samavai arranged for two. Other devotees made endowments for at least eleven more which have been recorded in 1551. Till recently there were four : in the month of Purattaasi, on Ratha saptami day, on Kaushika ekadashi in the month of Kartika and on Mukkoti ekadashi day. Today only the Purattaasi Brahmotsava is celebrated in September-October.

This Brahmotsavam goes on for eleven days. Before the festival, the garba griha and the small shrines are cleaned with a paste of sandalwood, camphor, saffron and other spices, a ritual known as Kovil Alvar Thirumanjanam. The day before the commencement is Mritsangrahanam, or collecting the earth when the temple officials pray to the minor deities Vishwaksena, Ananta, Sudarshana and Garuda for the successful conduct of the festival. They also collect some earth and sow nine varieties of grains (nava dhaanya). Thereafter, the head priest hoists the Garuda flag on the Dhvajastambham in a ritual known as the Dhvajaarohanam.

Every morning and evening the gorgeously bejewelled utsava murtis of Venkatesha, Sridevi and Bhudevi, are taken out in procession through the streets around the temple and then bathed in herbal water (Snapanam Thirumanjanam). The vehicles (vahanas) which carry the utsava murtis every evening for ten days are the snake Sesha, Hamsa, Simha, Punya koti, Garuda, elephant, Chandra prabha, Ashwa, ivory palanquin and Tiruchi (a palanquin). During the night, the utsava murtis of Venkateshwara and his consorts are kept in the Kalyana Mandapa.

Chandra prabha vahana – the moon as Balaji's vehicle

On the fifth day the deity is carried on his vehicle Garuda, the car festival (Ratha utsavam) takes place on the eighth day, when the makarakanti jewel and the Lakshmi haram worn by the main deity are used to adorn the utsava murti. On the ninth day the deity is bathed in sandalwood paste (Choornabhishekham) which is then distributed to the devotees. The tenth day is the Chakrasnanam when Balaji, his consorts and Sudarshana, the personification of his weapon Chakra, are bathed in the temple tank. On the last day, Sudarshana Chakra is bathed in the Swami Pushkarini, and Brahma, the Gods and the rishis are given a warm send-off.

Pavitrotsavam : Instituted by Saluva Narasimha, it is a purification rite conducted for five days commencing on Shukla dashami day in the month of Shravana.

Sarva Bhoopala Vahana — Krishna killing the demon Bakasura

The images decorated for the Pavitrotsavam

99

Balaji dressed as the deity Saraswati

Adhyayanotsavam : Conducted on Mukkoti Ekadashi day, the Vedas and the Tamil Divya Prabandhams (songs of the Alvars) are recited for twenty days. The utsava murti is kept in the Kalyana mandapa during this period.

Vasantotsavam : This spring (vasanta) festival is celebrated for four days between the asterisms Uttarabhadra and Krithika in the month of Phalguni.

Nityotsavam : It is performed for forty days after Ugadi, the Telugu New Year.

Thiruppali odai thirunal : This five day float festival honours the dancing image of Krishna and that of Rama on the first two days and the Utsava murti of Balaji, Sridevi and Bhudevi on the last three days. The deities are decorated and taken out on a boat (theppam) on the Swami Pushkarini.

Pushpa pallaki in July and **Pushpa yaagam** in November : During these festivals, flower-decked floats carry the utsava murtis around the temple town of Tirumala.

Those sevas and utsavams which are performed within the temple precincts can be observed only on payment of a fee. While this may seem unfair, it is unavoidable due to the circumstances in which the temple is situated.

From time immemorial, local tradition explicitly states that Venkatesha is standing on the hill, waiting to collect enough money to pay off his debt to Kubera. One of the meanings of his name Venkatesha is "Lord of the burning debts". Therefore the tradition of donating money to perform the utsavams is as old as the temple, from literary and inscriptional evidence.

Pushpa yaagam, floral offerings to Balaji

Pushpa pallaki, flower-decked float to carry Balaji

The utsava murtis decorated in pearls and gold

The practice of levying fees for every activity was born out of necessity in 1724, when Asaf Jah, Nizam of Hyderabad, appointed Daud Khan as Nawab of Carnatic. The latter demanded two lakhs of rupees annually as subsidy to leave the temple alone, an amount which had to be raised from the visiting pilgrims. The Nawabs of the Carnatic regularly levied heavy taxes. The practice of compulsorily charging fees was non-existent till the Muslims took over the region.

Today all the income from the fees goes to maintain the many charities and educational institutions of the Tirumala Tirupati Devasthanams.

The dharma darshan is free and open to all, even if the crowds make it slow and long. The Devasthanam authorities have built covered sheds with chairs and other facilities such as drinking water fountains, coffee, tea and food and adequate toilets for the comfort of the pilgrim as he slowly moves forward with the assembled crowds.

The annual festivals are the time for public celebration, when the utsava murtis are taken in splendour out of the temple and through the streets of Tirumala. It is a time when the Lord goes out of the temple to meet his devotees.

Balaji decorated with pearls

101

Hundi

The hundi is a tall collection bag in which pilgrims place their offerings. It is believed that Adi Shankara, who lived before the 7th century A.D., consecrated the Shri Chakra given by Lord Shiva beneath the hundi, hence its power to grant wealth. However, as the Shri Chakra is actually consecrated before the image of Goddess Kamakshi in the Kamakshi temple at Kanchipuram, there is another theory, that the Shyamantaka Mani of Lord Krishna is situated beneath the hundi, hence its power.

Pilgrims offer whatever they can afford into the hundi, circumambulate it and pray to Venkatesha in the hope and belief that he will reward them in return. The Lord always does, only we often cannot recognise his method of doing so.

There are many tales of the power of Balaji's hundi, of promises made and broken, only to be redeemed by the hundi. A businessman promised to drop his diamond ring into the hundi in return for Balaji's favour. When the time came, he decided to give the cash equivalent instead. But as he dropped the money into the hundi, he felt a powerful force pull off his ring. The story of the pious lady and the mangal sutra (page 16) is among the many instances when the power of the hundi has been evident.

Tonsure

A new visitor at Tirumala will find the sight of so many shaven heads most amusing. In fact the practice of shaving off all one's hair as an offering is so associated with this temple that a bald-shaven headed man is often asked whether he has had a "Tirupati mottai". Among some castes, young married women also shave off their hair, while babies and young boys visiting Tirupati invariably have shaven heads. The question one naturally asks is — Why?

The hair, in Indian tradition, is the most beautiful part of one's anatomy, hence the long, raven-haired women and men with a thick black head of hair. By tonsuring one's head, the last vestiges of ego (ahankara) are supposed to be abandoned, leaving the devotee naked and humble before the Lord. However, it is doubtful if most of those tonsuring their hair at Tirupati are aware of this.

The shaven hair is cleaned, made into wigs and exported. It is a little-known fact that the Tirumala temple is the world's largest exporter of human hair and wigs. The money earned is used for the TTD's many charities.

The sight of so many shaven heads can be quite amusing. To lessen the effect of the sun's heat on the bald plate, sandalwood paste is generally applied, giving the head a bright yellow colour.

The original image of Balaji —
Venkateshwara as seen in the
garba griha at Tirumala;
photographed in 1954.

Prayers to Balaji — Venkateshwara   Chapter 11

Special shlokas have been composed in celebration of Venkateshwara. They are recited regularly every day inside the temple and at home by the devotees.

Sri Venkatesha Suprabhatam

These are the shlokas or invocations with which the rituals for Venkateshwara begin in Tirumalai. They are also recited by the devotee during his daily prayers. They are made up of four parts :

Suprabhatam : literally, "good morning" or "a good dawn to you", a prayer awakening the God early in the morning. It is made up of twenty-nine stanzas, the first four addressed to Rama, Govinda (Krishna) and Shri or Lakshmi. The next twenty-four stanzas eulogize Venkatesha and address him by his various names. The last stanza says that whoever recites it every day will get happiness, peace and the highest state of moksha or final liberation.

Stotram : or "entreaty". Made up of eleven stanzas, the devotee prays for Venkatesha's protection, saying that as he comes from far away to worship at the Lord's feet, his occasional visits and adoration may be favoured with the same rewards as those received from daily worship.

Prapatti : meaning "surrender", this sixteen-stanza prayer to Venkatesha starts with a salutation to Shri-Lakshmi who resides on his chest, and goes on to surrender at the feet of the Lord. In the tenth stanza it refers to the Rig Vedic description of Vishnu's feet as the most exalted place of attainment, and in the eleventh to the Bhagavat Gita where the Lord, as Parthasarathi, showed Arjuna his feet as the place for unreserved submission. The shloka makes the point that Venkatesha will protect the devotee who totally surrenders himself to the Lord.

Mangalashaasanam : meaning "a prayer for glory and auspiciousness", it promises that those who go to see Venkatesha will desire to stand in his presence forever and continuously gaze at his handsome and attractive form.

Besides these prayers, the **Venkatesha Ashtottara Shata namah**, or the one hundred and eight names of the God, are commonly invoked in prayer.

The **Sahasranama** or 1008 names of Vishnu are also invoked for Venkatesha.

During the walk up Tirumala hill, the compositions of several devotees are played through loudspeakers, ringing through the hills.

Copper plates containing keertans by Tallapakam Annamacharya

Songs of the Alvars

We have seen that some of the Alvars — Poygai, Bhutat, Pey and Nammalvar — have written about Lord Balaji. Other Alvars who have praised Venkatesha include Tirumalisai, Kulashekhara, Periya, Andal, Tiruppan and Tirumangai. The Alvars were devotees or bhaktas of Vishnu who wrote passionate verse in Tamil about their love for their Lord. They lived over a period of about five hundred years and each one visited the temples sacred to Vishnu. They described the beauty and wonder of each manifestation in poetry which forms the 4000 Divya Prabhandams.

Other Carnatic music composers who composed songs on Venkatesha include Tallapakam Annamacharya and Tirumalacharya, who composed 32,000 songs in Sanskrit and Telugu. Even today, his descendants sing his compositions during the Ekanta Seva. Saint Tyagaraja, Muthusamy Dikshithar, Purandaradasa, Veena Kuppier, Subbaraya Shastri, Tirupati Narayanasami Naidu and Papanasam Sivam are the others who praised him in Sanskrit, Tamil, Telugu and Kannada.

In recent times several audio and video cassettes have been produced, containing songs in praise of Balaji — Venkateshwara, including songs and prayers by the great vocalist of Carnatic music, Smt. M. S. Subbalakshmi.

Tallapakam Ara, the building where the keertans are preserved, with sculptures of Tallapakam Annamacharya and Tirumalacharya

Balaji — Venkateshwara has stood at Tirumala since the dawn of civilization, to save his devotees from the evils of Kali yuga. History cannot explain or record the power and capabilities of the God, the temple and the hill.

At the beginning of this book we asked two questions:
Who is this God? Why is he so beloved of all?
The preceding pages have tried to answer these questions.
But what draws the crowds, particularly the hordes of young people who wait patiently in long queues?

We live in a world of change, where values are threatened all the time, where people are questioning their role and purpose in life, even the necessity of life itself. Young people are desperately trying to retain their ideals, to prevent cynicism taking over their lives. Their confusion, and their search for permanent values, takes them to Lord Balaji on Tirumala hill.

Vishwaroopa or Universal form of Vishnu; calendar print

A Vishnu bhakta

Triumph of good over evil

Whenever Dharma is in danger, Vishnu manifests himself on earth to rid the world of the evil. As Varaha, Vishnu destroys the evil demon Hiranyaksha, who steals the knowledge of truth as it is documented in the Vedas, and settles on the sacred Tirumala hill. Again, as Venkateshwara, he destroys evil demons who threaten the existence of Dharma. The demons represent negative forces and actions which prompt us to deviate from the path of righteousness.

The destruction of evil and the triumph of good is central to all religions, particularly Hinduism. Balaji is a role model — a model of divine perfection to be emulated by human beings in their search for the divine. Salvation can be achieved by mortals if they follow the path of goodness, truth and righteousness, without deviation.

Triumph of hope

The miracles associated with Balaji make the impossible possible. The stories of these miracles have spread far and wide and, as more people hear them, they too desire to visit Tirumala. He helps rich and poor, weak and strong.

Through his miracles Balaji protects his devotees. Sir Thomas Munroe and Lord Williams could never visit the temple, yet they reposed hope in Balaji, and he did not let them down. He is omnipresent and omnipotent, transcending barriers of time and space. As Vishnu the all-pervading Protector, he identifies with every believer.

Thus Balaji represents the triumph of hope — as long as there is hope in the human heart, there is no place for despair. The impossible can be achieved. This is an important message for young people in these days of fast-changing situations.

Triumph of faith

Balaji is a focus for faith — his temples are found in the heart of every believer. He protects his devotees, he is an embodiment of love. Their total faith in him creates miracles, for there is nothing as potent as faith.

When Mother Earth sinks into the nether world at the time of the great flood, she does not lose faith, for she knows that Lord Balaji will come to her rescue. Balaji destroys the evil Hiranyaksha who stands in his way and re-establishes the earth. It is this total faith in the Supreme Being that is essential for our well being.

As the pilgrim enters the sanctum sanctorum, powerful vibrations emanate from the deity. The pure and absolute faith of the devotee who reposes absolute trust in his Lord creates vibrations that permeate the air. Finally, to reaffirm the power of Bhakti or devotion, the devotee is absolved of his sins.

Humility

Sudhama and Krishna

When the sage Bhrigu visits Vaikuntha, he sees Vishnu reclining on the serpent Adishesha with Lakshmi by his side, and kicks Lord Vishnu on the right chest, the abode of Lakshmi. Instead of losing his temper, Vishnu bows to the rishi and washes and presses the latter's hands and feet, apologizing for his inattention at the arrival of a guest. His humility — despite the fact that he is a God and his consort Lakshmi is angry at his humble behaviour towards the proud rishi — impresses the sage so much that Bhrigu informs the other rishis that Vishnu alone can give them salvation. Krishna, ruler of Dwaraka, washes the feet of his friend and visitor, the poor Brahman Sudhama, and eats the handful of puffed rice, which alone has the ability to satisfy his hunger.

When the devotee shaves off all his or her hair, it is an act of humility, to affirm that he has abandoned his ego and is humble before the Lord.

Vishnu teaches us that one is never too high to be humble. Whatever the consequences, humility must never be forsaken — it has its own rewards. Brahma's pride denies him devotees and worship. Shiva was inattentive and Bhrigu forsook him. Arrogance is an evil, and can only harm us.

Charity

Humility leads to charity. Nearly all the wealth of the Tirumala temple goes to support education for the young and the welfare of the sick and the handicapped.

Balaji stands on Tirumala collecting money to "repay" a debt. What is this debt? He collects money from the "haves" and helps the "have nots", through the many charities and educational institutions run by the Devasthanam. In reality, he is repaying our debt to society, making us give in charity.

Supporting the poor, the less fortunate and the handicapped is regarded as a duty in the Hindu religion. However, not everybody has sufficient time or money to help the needy. Thus when the devotee places his offering in the hundi, he is helping others less fortunate than himself and, thereby, thanking the Lord for his own happy situation.

Respect for the earth and nature

As Varaha, Vishnu rescues the Earth from the evil demon. The story of Venkateshwara and his marriage with Padmavati is a celebration of our wonderful earth, her very existence and her bounty, and represents the fusion of the earth with the divine.

Religion teaches us to respect all creation and the bounties of nature. At the Tirumala temple, one can obtain prasada in the form of saplings and make endowments to plant trees. Through the various Sri Venkateshwara Vanaabhivriddhi schemes, the public can participate in the Devasthanam's afforestation programmes and earn great merit. All life is sacred and conserving the environment is our duty — this is the message from the temple of Tirumala, one of the few centres of religion where merit can be earned through actually conserving trees and nature.

Values

In a fast-changing world, where values and beliefs change almost daily, where people and situations are often not what they appear to be, Balaji represents a rock of

Krishna raising Mount Govardhana and protecting all creation; Indian Miniature painting

stability and security, of unchanging definitions of right and wrong, good and bad. This is a source of reaffirmation for the old and strength to the young. He represents continuity, moral values and all that is good and beautiful.

The pilgrim visits his Lord with awe and total devotion. Balaji takes over one's sorrows and worries, nobody who visits the temple with love and total devotion comes back without reward, either mental or physical or spiritual. Everybody is rewarded — whether it is a devotee who receives the object of his desire or the transgressor who is repentful.

The message

Lord Balaji — Venkateshwara gives every human being the opportunity to lead a better life, the right to hope and keep faith. He teaches us the difference between right and wrong, humility and pride, he helps us to help the less fortunate and to give back to nature an infinitesimal fraction of what she has given us. Finally, he assures us that it is never too late to repent and ask for forgiveness, that even the most wicked sinner can change for the better. What makes him unique is that the miracles he performs have changed lives and brought out the best in people as they realize his divine power and grace.

It is all summed up in the mantra —

Venkataadri samam sthaanam
brahmaande naasti kinchana;
Venkatesha samo devo
na bhooto na bhavishyati

which means

There is no place equal to Venkatadri
in the whole universe;
A God equal to Venkatesha
has never been nor will be.

111

Padmavati Devi   Balaji — Venkateshwara

Glossary

Aarati	An offering to the deity
Abhaya	Fearless
Abhishekha	Ritual ceremonial bath of the deity
Antarala	Intermediate area
Ashram	Forest home of a *rishi*
Asura	Demon
Bhagavat Gita	The Song Celestial, Hindu philosophy as propounded by Krishna, incarnation of Vishnu
Chakra	Vishnu's discus
Darshan	View
Dharma	Righteous duty and conduct
Dhvajastambham	Flag post
Dola	Swing
Dwadashi	Twelfth day after the full or new moon
Dwaram	Doorway
Ekadashi	Eleventh day after the full or new moon
Gada	Vishnu's mace
Gangalam	Large vessel to hold water
Garbha griha	Sanctum of a temple
Gopura	Gateway
Hasta	Hand posture
Hundi	Money collection box
Itihasa	History
Kalasha	Sacred vase
Kalpa	a period of 4,320,000,000 years, measuring the duration of the world
Kalyana	Wedding
Kirita	Crown
Kundala	Ear-ring
Mahabharata	Sanskrit epic with Krishna as the primary figure
Makara	Crocodile
Mandapa	Pavilion/hall
Mangala sutra	A pendant and chain worn around the neck by married women
Manusamhita	Social laws as expounded by Manu in the 4th century A.D.
Mithuna	Loving couple
Moksha	Liberation of the soul
Mottai	Bald
Murti	Image
Naivedyam	Sacred food offered to the deity
Nidhi	Treasure
Oonjal	Swing
Padi	Step
Pooja	Prayer or ritual
Pradakshina	Circumambulation
Prakara	Enclosure
Prasadam	Sacred food
Purana	Ancient history
Pushpa	Flower
Ramayana	Sanskrit epic with Rama as the primary figure
Ratha	Chariot
Rig Veda	The first and the oldest Veda
Sahasranama	Thousand names
Saligrama	Fossilised shells sacred to Vishnu
Seva	Service or offering
Shankha	Vishnu's conch
Shayana	Reclining or resting
Shloka	Sacred verse
Shri Chakra	The discus of Shri or Lakshmi
Shyamantaka Mani	Solar gem sacred to Krishna
Silappadikaram	Tamil epic
Tamil Sangam	Early Tamil school of literature
Teertha	Sacred
Theppam	Water float
Tholkaappiyam	Ancient Tamil book of grammar
Toranam	Decoration over doorway
Tulasi	Basil plant, sacred to Lakshmi
Upanishad	Books of Vedantic philosophy appended to the Vedas
Utsava	Celebration
Vahana	Vehicle
Vaikhanasa Agama	School of Vaishnava philosophy
Vaikuntha	Vishnu's paradise
Vaishnava	Follower of Vishnu
Vastram	Cloth
Varada	Boon - giving
Vedas	Sacred books of the Hindus
Vimana	Temple spire
Vishishtadvaita	*Vaishnava* philosophy propounded by Ramanuja
Yojana	Indian measure of distance, 1 yojana = 16 kilometres
Yuga	An era: 4 yugas make a *kalpa*

Select Bibliography

- **Administration of Temples** by C. Anna Rao
  (Tirupati, 1995)

- **The Art and Iconography of Vishnu-Narayana** by Nanditha Krishna
  (Bombay, 1980)

- **The Hill-Shrine of Vengadam** by S.K. Ramachandra Rao
  (Bangalore, 1993)

- **Hinduism - An Introduction** by Shakunthala Jagannathan
  (Bombay, 1984)

- **History of Tirupati**, Vol. I, II & III by T.K.T. Viraraghavacharya
  (Tirupati, 1997)

- **108 Vaishnavite Divya Desams**, Vol. V, by M.S. Ramesh
  (Tirupati, 1997)

- **Sculpture Art of Tirumala Tirupati Temple** by K.V. Raman
  (Tirupati, 1993)

- **Sri Venkateswara** by P. Sitapati (Bombay, 1968)

- **Tamils Eighteen Hundred Years Ago** by V. Kanakasabhai
  (Delhi, 1979)

- **Tattvaloka**, Vol. XIV, No. 2,
  (Bombay, 1991)

- **Temples of Tirumala, Tirupati and Tiruchanur** by M. Rama Rao
  (Tirupati, 1997)

- **Tirumala Tirupati Devasthanams Inscriptions and Report**, Vol. 1 to 8
  (Tirupati, 1998)

- **Tirupati Sri Venkateswara** by Sadhu Subrahmanya Sastry
  (Tirupati, 1998)

- **Bulletins and Manuals** published by the Tirumala Tirupati Devasthanam
  over the years